PASSPORT
TO THE
BIBLE

*An Explorer's
Guide*

**24 Basic Bible
Studies for
Groups or
Individuals**

InterVarsity Press
Downers Grove, Illinois

InterVarsity Press
P.O. Box 1400, Downers Grove, IL 60515
World Wide Web: www.ivpress.com
E-mail: mail@ivpress.com

InterVarsity Press® is the book-publishing division of InterVarsity Christian Fellowship/USA®, a student movement active on campus at hundreds of universities, colleges and schools of nursing in the United States of America, and a member movement of the International Fellowship of Evangelical Students. For information about local and regional activities, write Public Relations Dept., InterVarsity Christian Fellowship/USA, 6400 Schroeder Rd., P.O. Box 7895, Madison, WI 53707-7895.

"The Big Picture" includes and adapts material from Paul Hoffman, Stanley Klassen and Bill Syrios.

Cover photograph: Micael Rutherford/SuperStock

ISBN 0-8308-1171-0

Printed in the United States of America ∞

Library of Congress Cataloging-in-Publication Data

15	14	13	12	11	10	9	8	7	6	5	4	3	2	1

10	09	08	07	06	05	04	03	02	01	00	99

Introduction: Exploring the Bible by Katie Rawson —————— 5

The Big Picture by Katie Rawson ————————————— 10

PART ONE: MEETING GOD by Jane Pelz

1 The God of Mystery *Genesis 1:1—2:3* ————————— 17

2 The God Who Is Near *Psalm 139* ——————————— 20

3 God *Is* Great *Isaiah 40:9-31* ————————————— 23

4 God's Promises *Deuteronomy 5:1-21, 28; 6:1-9* ———— 26

5 God's Standards *Luke 10:25-37* ————————————— 29

6 The God Who Wants Us to Seek Him *Acts 17:16-32* ——— 32

PART TWO: WHO AM I? by Thomas Sirinides

1 Made for Relationship *Genesis 2:4-25* ————————— 35

2 What Went Wrong? *Genesis 3* ——————————————— 38

3 What Is the Point of Life? *Ecclesiastes 1:12—2:26* ——— 41

4 Your Place in God's Family *Luke 15:11-32* ——————— 44

5 Where Does Evil Come From? *Mark 7:1-23* ——————— 47

6 Turning from Sorrow to Joy *Psalm 32* ————————— 50

PART THREE: GOOD NEWS! by Terrell Smith

1 Good News for the World *Luke 2:1-20* ————————— 53

2 Good News for Sinners *Mark 2:1-17* —————————— 56

3 Good News About Evil *Mark 9:14-29* —————————— 59

4 Good News About Life *John 10:1-21* —————————— 62

5 Why Did Jesus Die? *Luke 23:13-25, 32-56* ——————— 65

6 Jesus Is Alive! *Luke 24:1-53* ——————————————— *68*

PART FOUR: EXPERIENCING GOD by Craig Colbert

1 Responding to God *Luke 8:4-9, 11-15* ——————————— *71*

2 A Working Man Responds *Luke 5:1-11* ——————————— *74*

3 A Rich Person Responds *Luke 18:18-30* ————————— *77*

4 An International Visitor Responds *Acts 8:26-39* ————— *80*

5 A Military Officer Responds *Acts 10:1-48* ——————— *83*

6 An Outcast Woman Responds *John 4:1-30, 39-42* ———— *87*

The Final Word: Passport to Life by Katie Rawson ———— *90*

Suggestions for Leaders by Katie Rawson ———————— *93*

Leader's Notes ————————————————————————*100*

Introduction: Exploring the Bible

I was ready to take my first international flight—to France. I had completed the long walk to the gate and was seated comfortably, waiting to board the plane. Suddenly I heard my name being called on the public address system. I had left my passport at the airline ticket counter! I shook on the inside as I retrieved the valuable document. Without my passport I could not have completed my journey.

Just as a passport gets you into another country, this guide will get you into the Bible. Reading the Bible for the first time, or even the second, can be a little like traveling in a foreign country. Without a map or a guidebook, the reader can easily feel disoriented. This guide is intended to orient you to the Bible and help you get the most out of your explorations. But before diving into the studies, it will be helpful to think through attitudes which promote learning, find out a little about the cultures of the Bible, get an overview of the studies and consider how to use the guide in a group.

Why Explore the Bible?

Not all places on earth are tourist destinations. Similarly, not all historical books are eagerly read. The Bible has been attractive to "explorers" for hundreds of years because it offers

☐ an explanation of the origin of humankind and the universe

☐ a description of the relationship between humans and their Creator

☐ an account of how evil entered the world and why it continues to affect us

☐ a history of all that God has done to establish close personal relationships with humans

☐ instructions for establishing peace and harmony between people and between humans and God.

Whole civilizations have been established on principles that were taken from the Bible. Exploring this document has much to offer to the eager, alert traveler.

Tourist or Learner: The Importance of Attitude

I approached living in France with determination to learn as much as I possibly could. Much to the aggravation of my American friends, I decided not to speak any English at all! I kept a little notebook with me all the time to write down new words and cultural items and constantly questioned French people about things I didn't understand. I ate at student cafeterias, sometimes having no idea what I was eating. And I avoided places frequented by tourists.

I didn't know it then, but I was doing what is often recommended to new-culture learners: immersing myself in the culture. A tourist can enjoy exotic food and scenery and then leave. In contrast a culture learner is willing to stay awhile, be puzzled and keep on trying to understand. It was choosing the learner attitude that allowed my experience in France to change my life.

I recently interviewed twenty-eight persons from several different countries who have come to know God personally through following Jesus Christ. The Bible was a very important part of the journey for most of them. But almost all of them actively did something about their search for God while investigating the Bible. They prayed, asked questions and even tried to put the parts of the Bible they could understand into practice. The choice to be a learner changed their lives.

Don't be content to be a "tourist" and close the Bible the first or second time you don't understand something. God has promised to reveal himself to those who seek him. When something puzzles you, ask someone who has been reading the Bible longer than you have. Or ask God himself. God inspired the authors of the Bible's books. Just as French people were my best source of information about their culture, so God is the best cultural informant on the Bible.

Consider beginning your time of Bible reading with a prayer similar to the following:

God, I am seeking to know you. Please reveal yourself to me. Help me to understand your Word and see how it applies to me. Thank you.

I have challenged many persons to pray a prayer like this and have known many who had it answered.

The Cultures of the Bible

In some ways reading the Bible is like exploring a new country, but there are at least five variables that make reading the Bible a more complex experience.

1. The *message* is a story about God and his work in the world. History is viewed from God's perspective, not from a human perspective.

2. The *authors* of the Bible are more than historians or reporters. They are not neutral. They have a unique purpose—to write what God communicated to them.

3. The original *readers* of the Bible lived long ago and spoke Hebrew and Greek. The Bible addresses their concerns, questions and problems.

4. The *location* (Middle and Near East) and *time* (about 2000 B.C. to nearly A.D. 100) of the events in the Bible are distant from us.

5. The *cultures* of the Bible are varied and span 2,100 years of human history.

The first five books of the Bible describe people in a tribal or kinship culture. In these cultures family is more important than the individual, and face-to-face personal relationships are valued. People in tribal cultures often worship many gods.

In most of the other Old Testament books, including Psalms and Proverbs, and in the stories (or parables) Jesus told in the New Testament, peasant cultures provide the background. People in peasant cultures make their living from the land and usually have rulers and a royal family. Status is very important in these cultures.

The later New Testament portrays a more urban and commercial culture in which the individual is primary. Thriving centers of trade, athletic games, and investments are part of this lifestyle. It was in this context that the logically argued letters of the Christian missionary Paul were written.

Just as some tourists head for museums and others for the theater, your cultural roots and personal learning style may cause you to be drawn to sections of the Bible most similar to your own experience. That doesn't mean the other parts can't speak to you, but it may require some cultural translation.

A few readers may find that it all seems very "long ago and far away." What do we, who live in a post-industrial information age have in common with the people in the Bible? First, people are the same in every era. You will find that biblical people yearned for wholeness and peace just as we do. Second, biblical people understood that we know others in the context of both relationship and experience. One of the Hebrew words translated "know" speaks of the intimate knowledge a husband has of his wife. Describing his experience of God, a Jewish poet said, "Taste and see that the Lord is good" (Psalm 34:8). So you will likely find that we have much in common with biblical people.

A Preview of the Guide
This guide begins with "The Big Picture," which provides an overview of the Bible. Then the first set of studies addresses the question, "Who is God and what is he like?" The next section focuses on what the Bible has to say about humans and their relationship to God. The third section focuses on Jesus Christ, his identity and teaching. The final section explores how we can respond to what we have learned about God and how we can experience him personally. Groups may begin with any of the first three sections.

Each study has the following components.

□ A brief introduction to the theme is presented, with a question to get you started thinking about and discussing the topic at hand.

□ *Getting Oriented:* Important background information on the Bible text.

□ *Key Words:* Definitions of words and terms that have biblical and theological significance. Key words are listed only once in each section. Terms easily found in a dictionary are not included.

□ *Exploring the Passage:* Questions on the passage that allow you to observe the facts, interpret the meaning and apply it to your life.

☐ *Charting Our Course:* Application to our lives.

Using *Passport to the Bible* in a Group

As you anticipate exploring the Bible in a group, you may feel excited or fearful. Agreeing to a few guidelines will help everyone in your group get the most out of your discussions.

1. The leader is the facilitator of the discussion, but not the teacher. Look to the Bible text itself to respond to the questions.

2. Stay focused on the passage being discussed. Help the leader keep the discussion on track.

3. Be willing to share your ideas, observations and questions with everyone else in the group.

4. Keep in mind that some people speak up readily, while others prefer to think quietly for a time.

5. Remember that no question is too simple, too unfriendly or too difficult. Direct your questions to the passage being discussed.

6. When a question arises that is not related to the text being considered, decide how you can handle it later. Some groups may want to keep a "questions" list and plan later Bible studies around these questions. Others may ask one member to research a question and report about it briefly the following week.

7. Treat everyone in the group on an equal basis—everyone's views are important.

8. The discussion questions are based on the New International Version of the Bible (NIV). Group discussion will be easier if everyone reads from the same translation.

9. Help the leader begin and end on time. People return more willingly to discussion groups when they know their time will be respected.

The Big Picture

The word *Bible* comes from the Greek word *biblia,* which means "books." The Bible contains sixty-six books, written by at least forty different authors over a period of at least 1,500 years. The oldest book was written about 1400 B.C. or earlier. The last book was written about A.D. 100. When we read the Bible in English, we are reading a translation of material originally written in Hebrew (the Old Testament or first part of the Bible) or Greek (the New Testament or second part of the Bible). The events described in the Bible take place in the lands north and west of the Persian Gulf and surrounding the Mediterranean Sea.

Although the biblical books are written in different styles and reflect different cultural backgrounds, the authors believed that what they wrote was uniquely inspired by God; their words are God's message to all people.

The Two Testaments

There are sixty-six books on the "Bible at a Glance" chart. The first thirty-nine books, from Genesis through Malachi, are grouped in a section called *the Old Testament.* The last twenty-seven books, from Matthew through Revelation, are called *the New Testament. Testament* is another word for a will or covenant, a legally binding promise. The Old Testament describes God's covenants with the Jewish people and his promise to bless all nations of the earth through them. The New Testament shows how this promise was fulfilled in Jesus Christ.

Despite covering over 2,000 years of human history, the Bible has a theme that unifies all of its sixty-six books. The Bible tells us what God has been doing in human history and the purposes for which he created us. The Bible's story can be viewed as a drama in five scenes.

THE BIBLE AT A GLANCE

OLD TESTAMENT PERIOD | **NEW TESTAMENT PERIOD**

Timeline: Creation — 2500 B.C. — 2000 B.C. — 1500 B.C. — 1000 B.C. — 500 B.C. — 0 — A.D. 25 — A.D. 50 — A.D. 75 — Future — New Creation

Antiquity	Adam & Eve; The Flood
2000 B.C.	Abraham; Jacob — Father of Israel's Twelve Tribes
1500 B.C.	Moses
1000 B.C.	David & Solomon; Construction of Temple
500 B.C.	Most of the Prophets
0 – A.D. 25	Jesus' Earthly Life
A.D. 50	Paul's Missionary Activity
Future / New Creation	

Creation & Crisis
Genesis 1—11
God creates the world
Adam and Eve disobey
Sin infects all life
God promises a solution

God's Solution Unfolds
Genesis 11—Malachi
God chooses Abraham and forms a nation
Israel disobeys and loses her freedom
God promises a solution

The Solution Is a Person
Matthew—John
God sends Jesus
Jesus obeys God
Jesus dies and is resurrected

God's New Multicultural Community
Acts—Jude
God gives his Spirit and a new heart to all ethnicities; a new people of God is born

A Look into the Future
The Revelation
Beauty and harmony
All nations worship God
Jesus is king

---

39 OLD TESTAMENT BOOKS

The Law
(The first five books, which gave the Jews their ethical framework)
Genesis
Exodus
Leviticus
Numbers
Deuteronomy

Genesis 1—11
(The story of the creation of all life and the special creation of human life, disobedience, and the resulting consequences)

The Prophets
(Messages from God to the Jews through a spokesman)
Joshua • Judges
1, 2 Samuel
1, 2 Kings
Isaiah • Jeremiah
Ezekiel
Hosea • Joel • Amos
Obadiah • Jonah • Micah
Nahum • Habakkuk
Zephaniah • Haggai
Zechariah
Malachi

The Writings
(Comprised of three wisdom books, five scrolls and four historical books)
Psalms
Proverbs
Job
Song of Songs
Ruth
Lamentations
Ecclesiastes • Esther
Daniel • Ezra
Nehemiah
1, 2 Chronicles

Note: These books are chronological only from Genesis to Nehemiah.

---

27 NEW TESTAMENT BOOKS

The Gospels:
Matthew
Mark
Luke
John
(Accounts of the life of Jesus from four different perspectives)

Acts of the Apostles and the Epistles:
Acts • Romans
1, 2 Corinthians
Galatians • Ephesians
Philippians • Colossians
1, 2 Thessalonians
1, 2 Timothy
Titus • Philemon
Hebrews • James
1, 2 Peter • 1, 2, 3 John • Jude
(Accounts of the missionary activity of early Christian leaders, and their letters to new communities of Christians)

The Revelation
(God's revelation to John about the scope of history)

Scene 1: Creation and Crisis, Genesis 1—11

The Bible opens with the statement, "In the beginning God created the heavens and the earth." The point of the Bible's teaching is not to prove that God exists, but to teach us what God is like. The story of our creation is one of beauty and harmony. Everything God made was good. The first human couple, Adam and Eve, were created for relationship with God, to obey him and enjoy him as his children. The harmony God intended is seen in the picture of a garden beautifully described in Genesis 2.

The picture was ruined when Adam and Eve chose to disobey God. Their life of harmony was shattered—not only with God but inside their hearts, with each other and with the earth. The Bible calls this refusal to trust and obey God *sin*.

In choosing to disobey God, Adam and Eve chose to turn from God and live apart from him, acting according to their own wishes. Not only did this dishonor God but it separated them from the source of all life, and so they experienced spiritual death—and eventually physical death as well. Ever since, all humans have acted just as their original parents did, and so death, spiritual and physical, has become part of all human experience.

God's earth was afflicted by this deadly virus called *sin*. But God's love for his creation did not change; he promised a cure for sin. A child would eventually be born to a descendent of Eve. This child would take the punishment for sin on himself (see Genesis 3:15). The rest of the stories in this first part of the Bible show how God protected the earth from total pollution by sin.

Scene 2: God's Solution Unfolds, Genesis 12—Malachi

This section contains the beginning stage of God's plan to repair the damage done by human disobedience. Around 2000 B.C., God chose one human, Abram (later renamed Abraham), and promised that through his son and grandson God would form a nation: Israel. The Jews, Abraham's descendants through his son Isaac and grandson Jacob, would be God's special people to keep alive knowledge about him on the earth.

The stories of how God cared for Israel point ahead toward God's solution for the human problem. God dramatically rescued Israel from slavery in Egypt around 1500 B.C. This rescue was a picture of what he intended to do for all humans through Jesus, the Messiah, or deliverer, whom he would send. God also communicated his laws to their leader Moses so that they would know how to live healthy and harmonious lives.

Despite all God did, Israel's history reflects the human problem of distrust and rebellion toward God. When God first gave them their own land, they frequently turned from God's laws and did what was right in their own eyes. They were not content to live under God's rule. They asked for a human king in order to be like other nations. When their kings listened to God and followed his ways, they had peace and well-being, especially during the reigns of David and Solomon, around 1000-930 B.C.

God placed Israel among various world powers so that they could be a lighthouse to all earth's people. God's intention was that Israel would model the peace and wholeness that come when people obey God's words. When Israel's great King Solomon built a temple where people could worship God, he knew foreigners would pray to God there. The great queen of Sheba visited Solomon and praised his God (1 Kings 10:9).

But Solomon himself, who was supposed to be the wisest man in the world, began to worship other gods at the end of his life. As a result, after he died his kingdom was divided into two nations, Israel and Judah. Both nations were conquered and taken into captivity—Israel in 722 B.C. and Judah in 586 B.C.

God did not give up on the people; he sent special messengers (prophets) to teach them how to live and remind them that the Messiah would come. To one of these prophets, Isaiah, who lived around 700 B.C., God gave amazing pictures of this Messiah.

Scene 3: The Solution, Matthew—John

The New Testament continues the story of God's plan for his world four hundred years after the last book in the Old Testament. The first four books, or Gospels, announce the arrival of the Messiah. Each Gospel is named after its writer and describes the life, teachings, death and resurrection of Jesus Christ. *Christ* is the Greek word meaning "Messiah," the one first announced to Eve in

Genesis and then to the Jewish people through the prophets.

Jesus taught that people could be born into God's family by believing in him. He also said that God's children should live in an attitude of love, serving others and forgiving even their enemies.

Jesus called twelve special men, the disciples or apostles, to be with him and tell others about him. But most of the religious leaders, including the leading priests and teachers of the Jewish law, did not listen to Jesus; they worked together to have him killed.

God's solution to the human problem of sin now became clear. Jesus, who never sinned, willingly died on a cross for the sins of all people who will look to him in faith. The punishment for sin is death, but God allowed Jesus to die for us as a substitute. Then Jesus was raised to life on the third day as a sign that he really is God's Son. Death was conquered and the power of sin was broken.

Jesus offers to give a new heart and a new spirit to anyone who will accept his gift of life. God forgives our sins, gives us his Holy Spirit to live inside us and promises us that we will be raised to new life with him after we die, not because of our own goodness but because of the goodness of Jesus. People may now once again live in harmony with God. (Jesus' death and resurrection occurred around A.D. 30.)

Scene 4: God's New Multicultural Community, Acts—Jude

Beginning with Acts we read the story of God's new kingdom people. They are equipped to carry on the work of Jesus. They tell all peoples that the King has come and that he invites them to join his new community. The books that follow are letters from leaders of the early Christian church.

The most famous of these leaders is Paul. Although he was a Jew, he obeyed Jesus' command to tell the good news to people who were not Jews. Paul saw himself as an ambassador of God, and he wanted people to be reconciled to God through Jesus (see 2 Corinthians 5:20). Paul was beaten, shipwrecked and eventually killed because of his faith in Jesus. But at the end of his life he was able to say, "I have kept the faith. Now there is in store for me a crown of righteousness" (2 Timothy 4:7-8). Paul wrote these words before he was killed in A.D. 67 or 68.

Scene 5: A Look into the Future: Revelation

The prophets or messengers of God in the Old Testament looked forward with hope to the return of the Messiah as King over everything. They thought it would all happen at one time when Jesus first came. Jesus taught that there are two comings. The first was God's coming to earth in the mission of Jesus to defeat sin and death. His second coming as King is still future. At that time God will remove all people who will not accept his Son as King. Everything will then be restored to the beauty and harmony pictured in the Genesis garden. People of every nation, tribe and language will worship God together (Revelation 7:9-10). The book of Revelation describes the events surrounding the return and crowning of Jesus as King.

Part *One*
Meeting God

Jane Pelz

1 The God of Mystery

Genesis 1:1—2:3

What is the nature of the physical universe? What is its origin? These questions have captured the human imagination since the beginning of time. The ancient Chinese viewed the earth as a square; China, "The Middle Kingdom," was at the center, its rulers possessing a divine mandate. The Egyptians regarded the earth as the rectangular foundation for the universe; the Milky Way was the celestial twin god of the Nile. The Mesopotamians thought of the earth as a floating vessel covered with a solid dome that occasionally seeped rain. According to this idea, the gods originated *after* the formation of the universe and played no part in its creation; the universe arose from some impersonal power.

When Galileo peered through his telescope in 1609, several millennia of accumulated thinking about the earth had to be abandoned as false.

Recall when you first wondered about the origin of the physical world. What ideas did you have about it?

What did others teach you?

How have your ideas changed as you have gotten older?

Getting Oriented
Genesis means "beginning." The book talks about the beginning of the universe, the human race and Israel. Because it is not an exhaustive account, it leaves some questions unanswered. However, it is a foundation of Jewish culture. It is the first of five books called *The Law of Moses.*

 **Read** Genesis 1:1—2:3.

Key Words

1:2 **the deep:** water
1:20 **teem:** to be full of
1:22 **blessed:** favored, happy

1:24 **livestock:** sheep, goats or cattle
2:1 **vast array:** many forms of life
2:3 **holy:** set apart for God

 Exploring the Passage

1. What do we learn about God from 1:1-2?

2. What are we told here about how God created the universe?

3. What patterns do you notice in the story of God's creating work?

4. How do God's actions in 1:3-13 add *form* to the earth?

5. How do God's actions in 1:14-25 add *fullness* to the earth?

6. How is the creation of humans different from how God creates other things (1:27-31)?

7. What do you think it means that we are created "in the image of God" (1:27)?

8. What are the similarities between God's work of creation and the responsibilities he gives humans?

9. How is the seventh day different from every other day (2:2-3)?

10. Why do you think this story became a foundation of Jewish culture?

11. What does this story offer to people who welcome its words?

Charting Our Course

Compare the Genesis story with the other creation stories you thought about at the beginning of this study. How are they similar?

How are they different?

What aspects of God (as he appears in this story) appeal to you?

2 The God Who Is Near

Psalm 139

Some people think of God as an impersonal force or power. Some imagine a policeman ready to punish all who break his laws. Some say God is cold and far away; they clap their hands to awaken the gods when they enter the temple. Some believe God will give us what we ask if we pray hard enough or in the right way or make the correct offerings.

What do you think God is like?

Getting Oriented

Psalm 139 is written in poetic form by David, the great Jewish king. It is a prayer directed to God expressing David's personal experience with God. It was used in the public worship services of the Jewish people.

Read Psalm 139.

Key Words

v. 5 **hem:** enclose, draw together

v. 15 **frame:** body

v. 15 **secret place:** in this case, referring to a mother's womb

v. 15 **the depths of the earth:** poetically referring to a mother's womb

v. 16 **all the days ordained:** the length of our life on earth

v. 16 **written in your book:** refers to God's knowledge of our lives

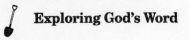 **Exploring God's Word**

1. List all the things we are told about God in verses 1-6.

2. What do all these statements about God have in common?

3. According to verses 1-4, what aspects of every human's life does God know about?

4. In verses 7-12 notice the vivid language David uses. What picture of God does he "paint" with his words?

5. How does it make you feel to read that we can't hide from God?

6. What more do we learn about how God looks at us from verses 13-16?

7. How does David respond to these insights about God (vv. 17-18)?

8. From verses 1-18 what does David believe about God?

9. In verses 19-24 there are two very different responses to God. Summarize each one.

10. We don't often invite others to search our secret thoughts. How do you explain David's invitation for God to do this?

 **Charting Our Course**

How have you seen evidence of God's involvement in your life?

How is David's view of God different from some of the pictures of God you described at the beginning?

In what ways would you like to know God more?

3 God *Is* Great

Isaiah 40:9-31

All of us search for significance and long for permanence. We want to leave behind some mark. Yet in reality very few will remember us.

What do you know about your great-grandparents? (For example, do you know where they lived? What were their characteristics and accomplishments?)

✗When your life ends, how would you like to be remembered?

Getting Oriented

Isaiah was a Jewish prophet who lived about 700 B.C. During this period Jerusalem was conquered by Babylon. Isaiah writes about the character and ways of God to comfort and encourage the Jewish exiles in Babylon.

 Read Isaiah 40:9-31.

Key Words

v. 9 **Zion, Jerusalem, Judah:** ways of referring to the homeland of the Jewish people; also references to the Jewish people themselves

v. 10 **sovereign:** all-powerful ruler

v. 10 **recompense:** payment, reward

v. 11 **breadth:** width

v. 19 **cast:** mold

v. 22 **canopy:** tent cover

v. 23 **naught:** nothing

v. 24 **chaff:** husk around a kernel of grain

v. 27 **Jacob:** another name for the nation of Israel

Exploring the Passage

1. List all the word pictures describing God in these verses?

2. Which descriptions surprised you or enlarged your understanding of God?

3. In what two ways is God's "arm" described in verses 10-11?

*Have you ever experienced God in either of these ways? Explain.

4. How would you describe the change in tone that begins at verse 12?

5. We have seen God compared to a ruler and a shepherd. Yet verses 18 and 25 imply that there is no comparison for God. In what sense is this true?

6. Idols are mentioned in verse 19. In your opinion, what is an idol?

Do you have any idols in your life?

7. What are some "idols" which do not have a physical shape?

8. Put verse 27 in your own words.

When have you felt like this?

9. In verse 27 a complaint is expressed. How does Isaiah answer the complaint in verses 28-31?

10. Reviewing the character of God expressed here by Isaiah, how would you describe the relationship God wants to have with us?

Charting Our Course

Look again at verse 31. On what do you base your hope for success?

What could keep you from putting your hope in the God described here?

4 God's Promises

Deuteronomy 5:1-21, 28; 6:1-9

Every culture has laws to govern human behavior. Singaporeans even wear T-shirts joking about their strict societal rules. Laws cover everything from traffic to property to violent acts. There are even international laws regarding trade and warfare. Some laws may seem frivolous; others are essential to peaceful coexistence.

What are some rules that governed your family as you grew up?

Which of these rules will you pass on to your children, and why?

Getting Oriented

Deuteronomy comes from the words *deuteros* meaning "second" and *nomos* meaning "law." The book repeats the moral law given earlier to Moses by God. This study includes that part of the law known as the Ten Commandments (5:7-21) as well as the *shema* (6:4-9), words still recited daily by Jews all over the world.

🕶 **Read** Deuteronomy 5:1-21, 28; 6:1-9.

🔑 **Key Words**

5:1 **summoned:** called

5:1 **decrees:** instructions, teachings

5:2 **Horeb:** mountain also known as Sinai

5:2 **covenant:** formal agreement, contract

5:12 **Sabbath:** seventh day of the Jewish week, a day set apart for rest and worship (Saturday)

5:18 **adultery:** sexual relations between a married person and someone who is not his or her spouse

5:21 **covet:** to desire something that belongs to someone else

6:5 **soul:** the innermost, nonphysical part of human life

Exploring the Passage

1. Describe how these laws came to the Jewish people (5:1-5).

2. How would you divide the laws in 5:7-21 into categories?

3. What can we learn about God from the behavior he commands?

4. From this passage, why do you think God is so particular about how the Jews relate to him?

5. According to 5:6-15, why does worship matter?

6. Examine 5:16-21. What are some benefits of following these commands, and what are some consequences of not following them?

7. In 6:1-3 what are we told about the purpose of these laws?

8. Following rules for the sake of rules has never been popular with most people. What is different about the motivation behind these laws?

9. Devout Jewish people recite 6:4-9 daily. What is the meaning of love for God as it is used here?

10 Sometimes people do the right things for the wrong reasons. What would be the wrong reasons for following these laws?

What would be the right reasons?

 Charting Our Course

❋ Look again at 6:6. How do laws travel from our heads to our hearts?

Would you say that these laws are mainly in your head or in your heart?

Why is this distinction important?

5 God's Standards

Luke 10:25-37

In this section we have explored passages that answer some of our most basic questions about God. Who is he? What is his relationship to the people of earth? What are his rules for living? Knowing that God has rules for us raises yet more questions: Does God grade on a curve? What does it take to get a passing mark? To explore these questions we move to the New Testament, to the parable (story) of the Good Samaritan.

But first, review your thoughts from the last study. What would you say is the difference between having laws in one's head and having them in one's heart?

Would you say that God is easy or difficult to live with? Explain.

Getting Oriented
In this passage Jesus tells a story to answer a challenging question that had a hidden motive.

🌱 **Read** Luke 10:25-37.

🔑 **Key Words**

v. 25 **eternal life:** the life that God gives to those who seek and love him; it begins now but will come to fullness after Christ returns to earth to judge and eliminate evil and to establish his rule as the perfect king over all the earth

v. 26 **law:** the rules given by God to the

Jewish people through Moses and found recorded in the first five books of the Bible

v. 30 **Jerusalem and Jericho:** two Jewish cities separated by 28 kilometers (17 miles) of mountainous and barren countryside

v. 32 **Levite:** Jewish priests had to be

descendants of Levi, one of the sons of Jacob, father of the twelve clans that formed the Jewish nation; not all Levites worked as priests, but they understood their role as preservers of morality and values.

v. 33 **Samaritan:** member of a mixed race of people that resulted from the intermarriage of Jews and foreigners over a period of seven hundred years. The Samaritans were regarded by the Jews as an impure race with a false religion; contact with them was avoided in order to preserve one's own ceremonial cleanness

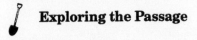

Exploring the Passage

1. Pretend that you are present on this occasion. What thoughts run through your mind and what feelings do you experience as the law expert stands and speaks (v. 25)?

2. How does Jesus avoid a possible trap?

3. Evaluate the law expert's answer (v. 27). As a requirement or standard for eternal life, what hope does it offer?

4. What does his second question reveal (v. 29)?

5. How does Jesus avoid getting stuck on legal definitions?

6. What in this story would have been surprising or disturbing for the law expert?

7. Who are the Samaritans in your world?

8. How do the actions of the Samaritan compare with those of the priest and the Levite?

9. How did Jesus define the meaning of "doing God's law" by telling this story?

10. What should the lawyer have come to understand about God's standards by the end of the story?

 Charting Our Course

The previous study on Deuteronomy 5 revealed God's ten laws for living. How does this study help clarify God's standards for how people should keep those laws?

Rethink your earlier answer to this question: In reality, is God easy or difficult to live with?

6 The God Who Wants Us to Seek Him

Acts 17:16-32

In our generation, seeking understanding of God can be like eating in a self-service cafeteria: there are a lot of choices! Many voices, both ancient and modern, offer their opinions and traditions as the right ones. It is tempting to conclude that there are many paths to God and people are responsible to choose for themselves.

How do you make sense of the many ideas about God in our world?

What difficulty do you see with the belief that there is only one path to God?

Getting Oriented

In this passage we meet Paul, a Roman citizen who was a Jewish Pharisee before he experienced a major change in his understanding of God. Paul has arrived in Athens (the intellectual capital of the world at that time). He finds the city full of religious expression, and he attempts to reason with its leading thinkers.

 Read Acts 17:16-32.

Key Words

v. 17 **synagogue:** a place where Jewish people met for worship and instruc-
tion in God's law

v. 18 **Stoic:** a person who believes that

human beings should be unaffected by pleasure and pain, calmly accepting whatever happens
v. 18 **Epicurean:** a person who believes that pleasure is the chief goal in life
v. 19 **Areopagus:** an assembly of

Athenians that, like a court, had authority in matters of religion and morality—especially over unknown preachers and teachers
v. 23 **inscription:** writing

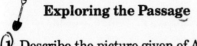

Exploring the Passage

1. Describe the picture given of Athens in verses 16-21.

2. The Athenians seem curious about the latest philosophies (vv. 19-21). Does this seem to be a positive or a negative thing? In what ways?

3. What convinced Paul that the people of Athens were very religious?

4. How does the God described by Paul in verses 24-31 differ from the gods of the Athenian people?

from opinions about God in our own societies today?

5. According to verses 26-28, what does God want from the people he has put on earth?

6. According to Paul, what should encourage people to seek God (vv. 27-28)?

7. Why is repentance a necessary step in coming to God?

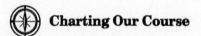 **Charting Our Course**

In what ways are you reaching out for God?

What are some opinions or views of God that you see are inadequate or misinformed?

Do you see anything about Jesus, "the man [God] has appointed" (v. 31), that helps you know God more fully?

Part Two
Who Am I?

Thomas Sirinides

1 Made for Relationship

Genesis 2:4-25

Western culture is very individualistic. Many other cultures—African, Asian, Latin, Arabic—are more group-oriented. Yet, in every culture people who want to be alone all the time are viewed as unusual. Humans need one another.

When do you most often feel the need to be with a friend or family member?

Getting Oriented

Genesis means "beginning." Chapter one tells the story of the beginning of all life forms. Chapter two focuses on human life and retells the story with more detail and insight as to the intended relationship between the Creator and humanity. The details about the garden which God made imply that it was a real place on the earth.

 Read Genesis 2:4-25, looking for connections between God and humans.

━● Key Words

v. 8 **Eden:** a specific place where the   v. 12 **aromatic resin and onyx:**
  Tigris and Euphrates rivers meet in   kinds of valuable gems
  southern Iraq   v. 19 **Adam:** a Hebrew word that
v. 10 **headwaters:** the beginning of a   means "man"
  river

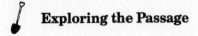 **Exploring the Passage**

1. Imagine how you would prepare if a member of your family was coming to visit you from overseas. How are God's actions in 2:4-9 similar to preparations you would make?

2. Why do you think God would do all this?

3. In 2:4-25 what information are we given about the first man?

4. In verse 15 God gave the man work to do. When you imagine the ideal world, is work a part of it? Why or why not?

5. In verses 16-17 God tells the man that there are limits to what he is allowed to do. What is the relationship between limits and love?

How might God's "No" here be a sign of his love for the man?

6. God has given the man life (v. 7), a home (v. 15), a job (v. 15) and limits (vv. 16-17). Now look at what God says in verse 18. Why might this be surprising?

7. Compare the description of the creation of the woman (vv. 21-22) with the description of the creation of the man (v. 7). What seems significant about the two descriptions?

8. What do you learn about what God is like from reading about how he has provided for the man?

 Charting Our Course

In Genesis we see that God has provided a rich environment for human life. From this reading, what expectations for life do you think God would want you to have?

How does this help you understand your feelings of loneliness and your desire to "connect" in relationships?

2 What Went Wrong?

Genesis 3

People have always wondered about the origin of pain and suffering. We ask, "If the world was once perfect, what happened?" The Bible says that we were made for close, loving relationships with God and with each other, yet we experience loneliness and alienation. And many of our countries are torn apart by war after war.

From your perspective, why does such suffering occur?

Getting Oriented

The narrative of Genesis 3 has moved from the big picture of Genesis 1 to the narrow setting of a garden. The literary style has changed as well, but the story continues to be historical rather than parable or myth.

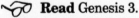 **Read** Genesis 3.

Key Words

v. 1 **serpent:** snake, often symbolic of Satan, the most powerful evil spirit

v. 1 **crafty:** skillful at deceiving others

v. 1 **garden:** the garden of Eden described in 2:8-14

v. 14 **cursed:** punished

v. 15 **enmity:** hatred

v. 18 **thorns and thistles:** weeds that are hard to remove

v. 24 **cherubim:** angels in the service of God

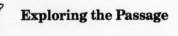 **Exploring the Passage**

1. How is the serpent described?

How do the serpent's words reveal his character?

2. How do God's words (2:16-17) compare with what the woman said about God (3:1-3)?

3. What might the woman's statement in 3:1-3 reveal about her attitude toward God's command?

4. In verses 4-5 the serpent is very direct. How does he paint an appealing picture for the woman?

5. What apparently motivated the woman to eat (v. 6)?

6. How did eating the fruit affect the humans' attitude toward themselves, each other and God?

7. Think about a time when you seriously hurt another person or were hurt by someone. How did it affect the quality of your relationship?

8. Name several ways that the first humans failed to trust God. How have these same steps caused pain, alienation and even wars in our own generation?

9. What actions does God take in verses 21-24?

In what sense are these actions of kindness?

10. In verses 14-15 God also takes action against the serpent. What has God promised to do to rid his creation of this source of broken relationships?

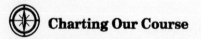 **Charting Our Course**

The story of the garden is also our story. Like the man and woman in the Bible, we have all made choices we regret. The story has a sad yet hopeful ending. God could have cut off contact with his creation. Instead he promises to deal with evil in a final and decisive act. God offered hope to the man and woman. He offers hope to us as well.

How has this story helped you to understand your experiences?

What has this story shown you about God?

3 What Is the Point of Life?

Ecclesiastes 1:12—2:26

Someone has said, "There are two significant moments in every person's life: the day you are born, and the day you discover *why* you were born." Most of us do not live our lives with such a long-range perspective. Many times our personal lives are just a collection of short-term goals (get my degree, get a job and so on) without any overall sense of purpose.

How would you complete this sentence: "My purpose in life is . . ."?

Getting Oriented
The title of the book of Ecclesiastes is a Greek version of a Hebrew word that means "the Teacher." Ecclesiastes contains the words of "the Teacher," a person who lived more than nine hundred years before Christ. He was, in fact, the third king of Israel, and his name was Solomon. King Solomon was known as the wisest man on earth.

 Read Ecclesiastes 1:12—2:26.

Key Words

1:16 **Jerusalem:** site of the king's home and of the temple of God

2:8 **province:** a section of a country

2:20 **toilsome:** exhausting

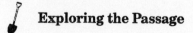 **Exploring the Passage**

1. What does Solomon tell us about himself in 1:12-18?

2. In 2:1-10 Solomon pursues the meaning of life by seeking to have fun, enjoy himself and find great success. What things did he try?

3. If Solomon lived today, what might be added to the list of things he did in order to enjoy himself?

4. In verse 12 we see that Solomon next considered wisdom and learning in his quest for meaning. What made education an attractive goal at first?

Why did Solomon eventually change his mind?

5. Having considered pleasure and education, Solomon next thinks about work. What does he conclude in 2:17-23?

6. Do you share his feelings? Why or why not?

7. In 2:24-26 what conclusions does Solomon draw?

8. Solomon continues his quest for life's purpose throughout the book and then sums up his thinking at the end of his book (12:13-14): "Fear God and keep his commandments, for this is the whole duty of man. For God will bring every deed into judgment, including every hidden thing, whether it is good or evil." From what we have studied in Ecclesiastes, how do you think Solomon would complete the question: "My purpose in life is . . ."?

What fears or questions does his answer raise for you?

 Charting Our Course

Solomon concluded that any pursuit in life would ultimately lead to frustration and disappointment. He knew this was true because he had pursued so many different things. What is your purpose in life? (What are your dreams, your goals, your aims—for this life, this year, this week, this day?)

4 Your Place in God's Family

Luke 15:11-32

Some studies claim that your position in the family will affect your personality. The firstborn child tends to be dutiful and disciplined. The middle child tends to focus on pleasing others and keeping the peace. The youngest child tends to be more carefree and even irresponsible.

What is your place in your family? How do you think that has affected you?

Getting Oriented

This story is probably the most famous that Jesus ever told. It is one of three stories Jesus told to answer those who criticized him because he associated with people considered to be sinners and irreligious. Each story describes something that was lost and the joy that resulted when it was found. These stories are called *parables:* stories of earthly life that teach spiritual truths by analogy.

🕶 **Read** Luke 15:11-32.

🗝 **Key Words**

v. 12 **estate:** property and money which is inherited when the owner dies

v. 13 **squandered:** wasted

v. 15 **feed pigs:** degrading work because Jews considered pigs to be unclean both physically and religiously

v. 18 **against heaven:** against God

v. 22 **robe, ring, sandals:** the robe signified honor, the ring symbolized authority, and sandals were worn by freemen (not slaves)

Exploring the Passage

1. What are your impressions of the younger son as this story begins?

What do you think are some of the reasons for his actions?

2. What qualities do you see in the father as he grants the son's request?

3. Are the father's actions what you would expect? Why or why not?

4. At what point does the son begin to change and why?

5. Contrast the son when he left with the son when he came home. How has his attitude about himself changed?

his attitude about his father?

his attitude about his own life?

6. What do you learn about the father from his response to the son's homecoming?

7. Describe the picture you are given of the older brother. How do you explain his reaction?

8. How would you describe the older brother's attitude toward himself, his father and his brother?

9. What do you learn about the father from the way he responds to the older son?

 **Charting Our Course**

We are all somewhat like one of these two brothers. Both were seeking fulfillment—one by declaring his independence, and the other by trying to meet the expectations of his father. Which of these two are you more like?

Both brothers failed to find satisfaction. One eventually came to his senses and returned home. The other never left home, yet he did not have the experience of the father's love. What barriers keep you from experiencing God's unconditional love?

5 Where Does Evil Come From?

Mark 7:1-23

The evening TV news is a source of despair for many people. Problems seem to dominate. We view self-serving athletes, disrespectful school children, dishonest businessmen, untruthful politicians, power-hungry heads of state. The problems go on and on.

What would you say is one serious problem facing your country, and what would you propose as a solution if you were in charge?

Getting Oriented
Mark's Gospel is the earliest written account of the life and teachings of Jesus. The author was not one of Jesus' original twelve disciples, but he was a companion of both Peter and Paul, two of the most prominent of Jesus' followers. In this reading Jesus is accused of violating established traditions of right and wrong. This leads to a fascinating analysis of the human problem.

∽ᗡ **Read** Mark 7:1-23.

━● **Key Words**

v. 1 **Pharisees:** religious leaders who stressed keeping every small detail of the Law of God and made new rules to cover situations not specifically mentioned

v. 1 **teachers of the law:** experts in interpreting details of God's Law and applying it to human situations

v. 2 **disciples:** people who follow a teacher, often "the twelve disciples," referring to the twelve men Jesus specially chose

v. 3 **ceremonial:** having to do with a custom that has symbolic meaning

v. 5 **unclean hands:** religiously impure hands

v. 6 **Isaiah:** a Jewish prophet who spoke
words from God (around 740 B.C.)

v. 6 **hypocrite:** a person who pretends
to be what he or she is not

v. 10 **Moses:** the writer of the first five
books of the Old Testament, which
contain the Law of God

v. 17 **parable:** a story of earthly life
which teaches spiritual truth

v. 21 **adultery:** sexual relations
between a married person and
someone who is not his or her spouse

v. 22 **folly:** foolishness

Exploring the Passage

1. How do the practices of the Pharisees and teachers of the law differ from the practices of Jesus and his disciples (vv. 1-4)?

2. What is Jesus' response to the Pharisees' complaint in verse 5?

3. Sometimes people who think they are worshiping God are actually only following the traditions of humans. How do you think people fall into such an error?

4. The Jewish people of Jesus' time believed that evil was something outside of themselves and that by careful living—including washing and eating correctly—they could keep themselves free from sin. How is Jesus' idea of what is ceremonially unclean different from what the Pharisees and the teachers of the Law see as unclean?

5. What are some ways people today emphasize outward actions over internal reality?

6. Jewish people distinguished themselves from other races by their observance of centuries of tradition. How does Jesus' standard for uncleanness cut through all racial distinction?

7. In your culture what traditions do people practice to give themselves the feeling that they are accepted by God?

8. Look at the listing of evils in verses 21-22. Jesus says that all acts originate in the human heart. Think back to our opening discussion about how we would solve some problems in the world today. If what Jesus said in verse 20 is true, how well would those solutions work?

9. What does this say about how we should deal with our own evil thoughts and attitudes?

Ezekid 76:25-29a

 Charting Our Course

~~Politicians, social scientists and educators all work to improve~~ human society. Yet eliminating poverty, unemployment or ignorance will not create good behavior. Parents have never needed to teach a child to lie or to be mean. Jesus' teaching confronts us with a crucial reality. We are not good people who sometimes yield to external forces of evil. Instead, we are all infected by a condition which makes us serve ourselves: selfishness. The Bible calls this *sin.* How do you respond to this description of our hearts?

6 Turning from Sorrow to Joy

Psalm 32

Part of having relationships with others is sometimes feeling pain—and sometimes causing pain for others.

Recall a time when you did something that clearly violated the wishes or values of your parents. How did it affect your relationship with them?

What did you have to do to repair your relationship?

◔ Getting Oriented

The Psalms are the prayer book of the Bible. They record in poetic form the experiences and emotions of real people. They are expressions from the heart directed to God by people who had personal relationships with him. Sometimes they are cries of despair, sometimes cries of anger, sometimes cries of joy. Always they are refreshingly honest. This psalm was written by David, one of Israel's greatest poets and its second king.

 **Read** Psalm 32.

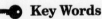 **Key Words**

v. 1 **transgressions:** acts which violate God's laws

v. 4 **sapped:** made weaker; reduced or diminished

v. 5 **iniquity:** wrong-doing; sin

v. 6 **mighty waters rise:** an image for times of trouble

v. 9 **bit and bridle:** equipment on a horse's head for controlling and directing it

v. 10 **woes:** sorrows   morally pure
v. 11 **upright:** doing what is right;

 Exploring the Passage

1. In verses 1-2 the word *blessed* could also be translated *happy.* What are the sources of happiness described here?

2. In verses 3-4 David remembers what his life was like before he was forgiven. What words in these verses describe him at that time?

3. Examine verses 1-5 for words of "cause and effect." What happened to the writer and why did it happen?

4. What here surprises you, and what seems reasonable?

5. In verses 6-11 what warnings does David offer to help us avoid the difficulties he went through?

(open?) Someone knows everything about you

6. Many people fear exposing and confessing their sin, yet David expresses a sense of protection and safety in making his confession. How can that be?

vs 10 →

7. What promises from God does David give (vv. 6-11)? What are the conditions?

8. Why might it be hard for people to act on these promises? (Hint: What makes it hard for *you* to admit when you have been wrong?)

⊕ Charting Our Course

Like the writer of this psalm, we often act "like the horse or the mule" (v. 9). We stubbornly refuse to let go of our own ideas, to admit our limitations or to confess that we have been wrong. Yet, as David has shown us from his own life, when we are willing to do these things, true happiness will become ours. This writer's realization of his need to turn to God is an example for us all.

What changes does this study prompt you to make in your life?

If you feel ready, take some time in private to write out your own confession to God.

Part Three
Good News!

Terrell Smith

1 Good News for the World

Luke 2:1-20

We might think the birth of someone as famous as Jesus would be rather unusual. We would expect someone like him to be born in a king's palace, and news of his to birth be carried by messengers to everyone in the kingdom. The facts of Jesus' birth, however, are quite different, as we shall see.

Consider the events surrounding your own birth. What has your mother or father told you about it?

What was happening in the world at the time of your birth that affected your family?

Getting Oriented

Jesus' birth took place about two thousand years ago in a small town called Bethlehem, about eight kilometers (five miles) south of Jerusalem, in the province called Judea, in the Middle East. This area was part of the Roman Empire, which included the area around the Mediterranean Sea, some of Europe, and North Africa. Caesar Augustus was the powerful ruler of the Roman Empire from 27 B.C. until A.D. 14. Quirinius was governor of Syria, possibly from 10 B.C. until A.D. 9. Because of a calendar adjustment, the time of Jesus' birth was probably in the year now designated as 4 B.C.

〜⌒ **Read** Luke 2:1-20.

━━● **Key Words**

v. 1 **census:** the counting of all citizens
v. 4 **Nazareth:** a town in the province of Galilee about 115 kilometers (71 miles) north of Bethlehem
v. 4 **house and line of David:** descendants of David, a shepherd who ruled as one of the greatest kings of Israel around the years 1011 to 971 B.C.
v. 7 **manger:** a feeding box for animals

v. 9 **angel of the Lord:** a heavenly messenger sent by God
v. 9 **glory of the Lord:** the awesome revealing of who God is, his being, nature and holiness
v. 11 **Savior:** one who delivers, frees, saves from danger
v. 11 **Christ:** the Greek word translating the Hebrew title *Messiah* meaning "the chosen one"

Exploring the Passage

1. How would you describe the power and authority of the Roman ruler Caesar Augustus (vv. 1-3)?

2. According to verses 4-7 what challenges and difficulties does Mary experience?

3. The story now shifts (vv. 8-14) from the manger in Bethlehem to shepherds in nearby fields. What status do shepherds have in your society?

4. We can see in verse 9 that the shepherds were terrified by the angel. How would you have felt if you had been one of these shepherds?

5. In verses 10-14, what reasons does the angel give the shepherds not to be afraid?

6. God decided to communicate "good news of great joy" (v. 10) to the shepherds. What does this tell us about God?

7. After seeing Jesus the shepherds are eager to "spread the word concerning what had been told them about this child" (v. 17). Why do you suppose they are so excited?

8. According to verse 18 "All who heard it were amazed at what the shepherds said to them." What is amazing or special about Jesus' birth?

 Charting Our Course

From reading about the events surrounding the birth of Jesus, what do we learn about God's concern for our lives?

From the passage, what does God want everyone to know and experience?

2 Good News for Sinners

Mark 2:1-17

What is the heaviest load you have ever carried? Share the circumstances of this experience. Not all loads are physical. Some, such as sorrow, pain, guilt or shame, may be as heavy as a physical load but hidden from other people.

Recall a time when you struggled with a hidden load. Who or what helped lift the weight of that load?

What do you think is our greatest need?

Getting Oriented

Jesus has been going around the region of Galilee, demonstrating his power. He calls people to follow him, and they leave everything behind to do that. People are amazed at his teaching, because he teaches them with authority, unlike their own teachers of God's law. He even commands evil spirits to come out of people, and the spirits obey him. Sick people are made well again. Jesus is becoming very popular. Now Jesus returns to Capernaum, a town on the northwest side of the Sea of Galilee and is preaching "the Word," the message of God.

Read Mark 2:1-17.

Key Words

v. 3 **paralytic:** a paralyzed person, unable to move

v. 5 **faith:** trust; believing something is true and acting on it

v. 5 **sins:** actions that fall short of God's standards, missing the target

v. 5 **forgiven:** God's forgiveness means that payment for sins is made and the sins are removed

v. 6 **teachers of the law:** experts in

the Jewish religious law

v. 7 **blaspheming:** insulting the honor of God; assuming rights which belong only to God

v. 10 **Son of Man:** a name Jesus often used for himself taken from a prophecy made by Daniel in the sixth century B.C. of a heavenly being who will come and have ultimate power (see Daniel 7:13)

v. 14 **tax collector:** a Jewish person who worked for the despised Roman government to collect taxes from his own people, charging whatever he could get and keeping the profit

v. 15 **disciples:** people who follow a teacher, often "the twelve disciples," referring to the twelve men Jesus specially chose

v. 16 **Pharisees:** religious leaders who stressed keeping every small detail of the Law of God and made new rules to cover situations not specifically mentioned

v. 17 **righteous:** probably from an Arab word meaning "straightness"—a right relationship between a person and God

Exploring the Passage

1. What is Jesus doing that attracts so many people to want to be near him (vv. 1-4)?

2. Imagine yourself as the paralyzed man being lowered through a hole in the roof down into the crowd and in front of Jesus. What would your thoughts and feelings be?

3. How would you feel hearing the words from Jesus, "Son, your sins are forgiven" (v. 5)?

O Why are the Pharisees surprised by his words?

4. In verse 6 the teachers of the law ask, "Why does this fellow talk like that? He is blaspheming! Who can forgive sins but God alone?" Why does Jesus talk like that?

5. What does Jesus' answer reveal about himself (vv. 8-12)?

Why do you think Jesus forgives the man before He heals him? What does this say about Jesus.

6. Later Jesus goes out beside the lake (the Sea of Galilee) and as he walks along he meets Levi. Describe how Jesus gets involved in Levi's life (vv. 13-15).

What kind of person was Levi?

7. From verses 14 and 15 what do you think "following Jesus" means?

8. In verse 16 we see the teachers of the law are upset again by what Jesus does and they ask Jesus' disciples, "Why does he eat with tax collectors and sinners?" Why *did* Jesus eat with tax collectors and sinners?

Charting Our Course

People who recognize they are sick and who want to get well usually try to go to a doctor. The paralytic and Levi may seem to be very different. Yet how are they similar?

What are some ways we are similar to the paralytic and Levi?

What have you seen in Jesus that would encourage you to seek his help?

3 Good News About Evil

Mark 9:14-29

Some people don't think about spirits or about the power of evil spirits. Others have experienced strong influence from evil spirits in their own lives or the lives of family members or friends.

One morning at breakfast, a student from Asia said, "I couldn't sleep last night. There was an evil spirit screaming outside my door all night." If someone said this to you, how would you respond?

Getting Oriented
Jesus has been teaching and healing many people. He is especially focused on helping his disciples, his followers, to more fully understand who he is and why he came. Jesus is just now coming down from a mountain with three of his disciples to join the rest of the disciples.

👓 **Read** Mark 9:14-29.

 **Key Words**

v. 17 **spirit:** here an evil spirit, a supernatural being (not human), that can enter and control a person

v. 18 **foams:** produces bubbles of saliva around the mouth

v. 18 **gnashes:** grinds teeth together

v. 20 **convulsion:** violent, uncontrollable contractions of muscles

v. 25 **mute:** unable to speak

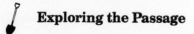 **Exploring the Passage**

1. How would you describe the situation at the beginning of this story?

2. When Jesus came back to the other disciples, they were arguing with some teachers of the Jewish law. Why do you suppose all the people left the lively argument and ran to Jesus (v. 15)?

3. What qualities of being human has the son lost by being possessed by the evil spirit (vv. 17-18)?

4. What are some spirits or powers that bind up people you know?

5. The evil spirit is trying to kill the boy, and the father is searching for help. Why do you think Jesus waits and asks so many questions before helping (vv. 19-24)?

6. List the ways that Jesus shows his authority over the evil spirit in verses 25-27.

7. In verses 28-29, Jesus' disciples ask, "Why couldn't we drive it out?" Jesus replies, "This kind can come out only by prayer." How do you define prayer?

8. What insights about prayer does the earlier conversation with the father (vv. 22-24) give us?

9. What is necessary in order to experience Jesus' authority in our lives?

 Charting Our Course

Think about a time when you felt powerless to change or control some aspect of your life. What encouragement does this father's experience give you?

4 Good News About Life

John 10:1-21

Some people appear to think only of themselves. Others are consistent in putting the needs of others before their own.

Think of someone who does things for his or her own gain. How far are people willing to go to make sure they succeed?

Now think of someone who is self-giving and loving. How far are such people willing to go to show love?

Getting Oriented

Jesus has been teaching and demonstrating who he is and why he came. In the section just before this reading (9:1-41), Jesus heals a man who was born blind. There are mixed reactions to what Jesus is teaching. Some people have stopped following him because they find his teaching too hard to accept (6:60). Others have been wondering, *Who is Jesus? Is he the Christ, the promised one?* (7:40-41). The religious leaders do not believe in him (7:48). Other people do believe (9:38). It is to this mixed group of people that Jesus gives his teaching of the shepherd and the sheep.

👓 **Read** John 10:1-21.

🔑 **Key Words**

v. 1 **I tell you the truth:** a formal saying indicating that what is about to be said is important

v. 6 **figure of speech:** a word or

expression that illustrates and
explains something

v. 9 **saved:** rescued from danger,
particularly on the coming day
of judgment

v. 15 **Father:** how Jesus often refers
to God

v. 20 **demon-possessed:** the state of a
person controlled by an evil supernatural (not human) being

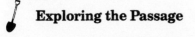

Exploring the Passage

1. From verses 1-6, how would you describe the relationship between the shepherd and his sheep?

2. In verse 6 we see that the people do not understand what Jesus
is telling them. What do you think Jesus is really saying?

3. Because the people don't understand, Jesus says it another way
in verses 7-10. What are the differences between Jesus and the
"thieves and robbers"?

4. In verses 11-13 we read about two kinds of shepherds. What are
the reasons behind the different actions of the good shepherd and
the hired hand?

5. In verse 14 Jesus repeats that he is the good shepherd. What
does the good shepherd do for his sheep (vv. 15-16)?

6. In verse 16 Jesus says, "I have other sheep that are not of this sheep pen." Who do you think Jesus is talking about? How does this make you feel?

7. Several times Jesus has said that he will lay down his life for his sheep (vv. 11, 15, 17-18). Why does the shepherd lay down his life for the sheep?

8. What do we learn about Jesus when he says he will lay down his life of his own accord and take it up again (vv. 17-18)?

9. We read in verses 19-21 that the people hearing Jesus were divided in their opinion about him. How would you answer those who asked, "Why listen to him?"

🧭 Charting Our Course

Jesus makes some strong and exclusive statements: "I am the gate [not just *a* gate]," "I am the good shepherd," "I have authority to lay down my life and take it up again," and so on. What will we experience if we listen to his voice?

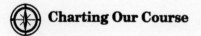

How could Jesus make your life more full this week?

5 Why Did Jesus Die?

Luke 23:13-25, 32-56

We don't like to think about death. Yet death is a fact of our human experience. We have all probably experienced the death of someone who was close to us.

What are some feelings you experience when thinking about death?

Have you lost someone who was close to you?. What was that experience like?

Getting Oriented

Some people believe that Jesus' death was a sad and sudden end to a wonderful life. They wonder why God didn't prevent it.

At the time of Jesus' death, Pilate was the harsh Roman governor (A.D. 26-36) of the territory of Judea, which includes Jerusalem. The chief priests and rulers served as a Jewish ruling body, permitted to have limited authority under the Roman authorities. Herod was appointed by the Roman occupying forces as King of the Jews over the territory of Galilee from 4 B.C. to A.D. 39. Jesus was betrayed by one of his disciples, arrested by the temple guards and forsaken by his followers, who ran away. He was mocked and beaten and then taken to the Roman authorities, Pilate and Herod.

👓 **Read** Luke 23:13-25, 32-56.

🔑 **Key Words**

v. 19 **insurrection:** rebellion, an attempt to overthrow the government

v. 21 **crucify:** to kill by a cruel means of execution practiced by the Romans.

The feet and outstretched hands of the person were nailed to a wooden structure made in the shape of the letter T. Then, with the nailed person hanging on it, the structure was stood vertically, its base in a hole in the ground. Death was caused by exposure, bleeding and suffocation and normally took two to three days.

v. 34 **casting lots:** a way of making decisions, like rolling dice

v. 36 **mocked:** made fun of

v. 43 **paradise:** from an Iranian word meaning "walled garden"; here it may mean "the walled garden of God"

v. 45 **curtain of the temple:** in the Jewish temple this hung in front of the most holy place, to keep the people from the holy place of God

v. 47 **centurion:** a Roman officer in charge of 100 soldiers

v. 48 **beat their breasts:** a way of expressing grief and sadness

v. 50 **Council:** the supreme court of the Jews

v. 51 **kingdom of God:** the place or condition in which people live under God's rule

v. 53 **linen:** a rich cloth used for special purposes

v. 54 **Preparation Day:** the twenty-four-hour period beginning at sundown Thursday to prepare for the yearly Jewish festival of Passover

v. 54 **Sabbath:** in the Jewish calendar, the seventh day of the week, beginning at sundown on Friday; a day devoted to God

v. 56 **commandment:** in this case the fourth of the Ten Commandments given by God through Moses: to rest on the Sabbath

Exploring the Passage

1. Both Pilate and Herod, after examining Jesus, conclude that there is no basis for the charges against him (vv. 13-15, 20, 22). Why do you think Pilate decided to grant the people's demand (v. 24)?

2. In verses 32-34 we read that Jesus was crucified with two criminals. Given his circumstances, what is surprising about the way Jesus prays (v. 34)?

3. In verses 35-39 the rulers sneer at Jesus, the soldiers mock him, and one of the criminals insults him. What is similar about all their comments?

4. The other criminal asks (v. 40), "Don't you fear God?" Why should someone in this situation fear God?

5. From the words this criminal speaks in verse 42, what would you say he believes about Jesus?

6. If this criminal is guilty and Jesus is innocent, how can Jesus say (v. 43) they will be together in paradise?

7. In verses 44-49 Luke records a number of unusual things that happened when Jesus died: darkness came over the whole land, the curtain of the Jewish temple was torn in two, the Roman centurion praised God and the people went away beating their breasts. What (or who) do you think caused all these changes?

8. In verses 50-54 Joseph asked for the body of Jesus. What risks was Joseph taking?

What does his risk-taking tell you about him?

9. What was the purpose of the spices and perfumes the women prepared (vv. 55-56)?

 **Charting Our Course**

✳ People had different opinions about Jesus, and some changed their opinions when they saw the way Jesus acted when he died. Which person in this story most closely reflects what you think about Jesus?

What risks might you face if you identify yourself as being interested in Jesus?

✳ What new understanding of Jesus' death have you gained?

6 Jesus Is Alive!

Luke 24:1-53

Sometimes unexpected things happen in our lives that really surprise us—especially when they are good.

What event in your life was such good news you could hardly believe it, was unexpected, or was a total surprise?

Getting Oriented

Although the Roman governor Pilate had declared Jesus innocent, he gave in to the shouts of the people, the chief priests and rulers, and allowed Jesus to be crucified, a cruel means of execution practiced by the Romans. When Jesus was dead, his body was wrapped in a linen cloth and placed in a tomb cut in rock which was sealed by a large stone rolled across the opening.

Read Luke 24:1-53.

Key Words

v. 6 **Galilee:** the province north of Judea where Jesus spent much of his life

v. 9 **the eleven:** the remaining followers of Jesus' original group of twelve (after Judas's death)

v. 10 **apostles:** the twelve individuals Jesus chose to be with him and carry on his mission

v. 13 **Emmaus:** a village about 11 kilometers (7 miles) west of Jerusalem

v. 19 **prophet:** one specially called by God to speak his truth

v. 20 **chief priests and rulers:** the Jewish ruling body given limited authority by the Romans

v. 21 **redeem:** to rescue by payment of a price

v. 27 **Moses:** leader who lived about 1350-1230 B.C., led the Jewish nation out of captivity in Egypt and wrote down God's laws for the people

v. 27 **Scriptures:** in this case the Hebrew Scriptures or "Old Testament," the words of God

v. 37 **ghost:** the spirit of one who has died

v. 44 **Law of Moses:** the first five

books of the Bible (one of three main
sections of the Old Testament)

v. 44 **the Prophets:** all of the writings
of the prophets in the Old Testament
(another of the three sections)

v. 44 **the Psalms:** the writings of David
and others (the third section of the
Old Testament)

v. 47 **repentance:** turning around and
changing one's mind and behavior

v. 49 **clothed with power:** energized
by God's Spirit

v. 50 **Bethany:** a village about three
kilometers (two miles) from
Jerusalem

v. 53 **temple:** the building in Jerusalem
where people came to worship God

Exploring the Passage

1. Early on the first day of the week, the women went to the tomb
(vv. 1-8). Contrast what the women were planning to do when they
got to the tomb with what actually happened when they got there.

2. The women went back and told all the others. What differences
are there in the way the women react and how the men react (vv.
9-12)?

3. Now the story moves to two men walking toward a village called
Emmaus. From verses 13-24, how do the men describe Jesus and
their hopes for him?

4. Jesus joins them and they finally recognize him (vv. 25-35). What
process did they go through before they could see and recognize
Jesus?

5. In verses 36-45 Jesus appears to the disciples. How does he invite them to answer their questions and doubts?

6. Jesus explains (vv. 46-49) that what has happened was exactly what was supposed to happen. According to Jesus, what can happen now because he suffered, died and rose from the dead?

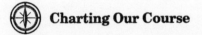 **Charting Our Course**

In this reading we have seen how three groups of people (women, two men, disciples) moved from doubt to faith. Which of their attitudes best represents *your* current thinking about Jesus?

What was common to each group's journey to belief?

What steps could you take to move toward understanding and faith?

Part Four
Experiencing God

Craig Colbert

1 Responding to God

Luke 8:4-9, 11-15

Jesus was a storyteller. He painted word pictures to help people understand about God and how people can relate to God.

Describe your history with the God of the Bible. When did you begin to hear his words?

What brought this about?

Getting Oriented
Because Israel was an agricultural culture, Jesus often used illustrations from the countryside. For 800 years the Jewish people heard their prophets teach that God would send a deliverer, or Messiah, who would be "God with us." Many Jews thought that when the Messiah came, all Israel would follow him. In this story Jesus indicates that there always have been and always will be various responses to God's words.

👓 **Read** Luke 8:4-9, 11-15.

⚊🔴 Key Words

v. 4 **parable:** a form of teaching in
which a story is used to illustrate a
main truth by means of comparison
v. 9 **disciples:** followers, usually
referring to the twelve men Jesus
chose to follow him
v. 12 **devil:** the most powerful evil
spiritual being

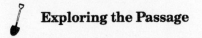 **Exploring the Passage**

1. Look carefully at verses 5-8. There are four different places
where the seed fell. What are the differences between the seed beds,
and what is the same in each situation?

2. After telling the parable, Jesus says, "He who has ears to hear,
let him hear" (v. 8). Why do you think it was his disciples who asked
for an explanation of the parable?

3. In Jesus' explanation of the parable (vv. 11-15) what is unique
about the first situation?

4. What are some ways the devil prevents people from even wel-
coming God's words?

5. How is the seed that fell on rocky ground an improvement over
the seed on the path?

6. What is the danger of making only an emotional response to God?

7. How is the seed that falls among thorns different from the seed falling on rocky ground?

8. What are some examples of "worries, riches and pleasures" that you have encountered which threaten to choke out the growth of God's words in our lives?

9. How is the good soil different from the other three seed beds?

10. What has Jesus said in this parable that throws light or understanding on your own experience with God's words?

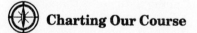 **Charting Our Course**

How does this parable explain the danger of doing nothing?

the danger of responding only with enthusiasm?

why following God sometimes creates conflict?

2 A Working Man Responds

Luke 5:1-11

Some men think that "religion" is for women and children. But many of Jesus' early followers were men who worked with their hands, typically in the heat of the day. Jesus invited hardworking men to follow him, changing their lives forever.

What has been the most significant change you have made in your life so far, and what happened to bring about that change?

Getting Oriented

Until the age of thirty, Jesus worked as a carpenter. Simon Peter was a working man, a fisherman by trade. He and his partners had spent all night fishing and now were washing and drying their nets prior to ending their day. Simon Peter's encounter with Jesus changed his life.

👓 **Read** Luke 5:1-11.

🔑 **Key Words**

v. 1 **Lake of Gennesaret:** another name for the Lake, or Sea, of Galilee

v. 3 **put out:** to launch a boat

v. 5 **master:** literally rabbi or teacher

v. 8 **sinful:** having broken God's laws, missed the target of his standards

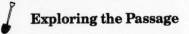 **Exploring the Passage**

1. In the middle of this crowd of people, what brings Jesus and Simon into contact?

2. How would you feel if a very famous person asked to borrow your car with you as the driver?

How might this compare to how Simon felt when Jesus spoke to him?

3. After speaking to the crowd, Jesus gives instructions to Simon (vv. 4-5). How are these words different from the request to move the boat offshore (v. 3)?

4. After following Jesus' instructions, Simon and his partners have an unusual catch (vv. 6-7). Why are they so astonished?

5. Simon's title for Jesus in verse 8 is different from verse 5. What has happened to his understanding of Jesus?

6. What has Simon learned about himself?

7. Simon understands that sin separates people from God, so he is frightened by God's part in this great catch. How does Jesus respond to Simon's fear?

8. Compare the cost and risk of acting on Jesus' words (v. 10) with the words of verse 4. Why do you think Simon and his companions respond without hesitation this time?

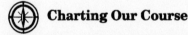 **Charting Our Course**

Notice how Jesus skillfully and gradually led Simon to discover that even in the areas of life in which Simon was the expert, Jesus knew more. What are those areas in your life in which Jesus may have something to say (like a teacher) but is not yet Lord?

3 A Rich Person Responds

Luke 18:18-30

Jesus calls people not just to discuss what he says, but to respond. Some choose to respond by following Jesus. For others the cost of commitment is too high a price to pay, and they respond to Jesus in a different way.

Think about the things you have achieved in life. What commitment did each achievement require from you?

What are some of your major commitments at this time?

Getting Oriented

This story is also told in Matthew 19 and Mark 10. Matthew tells us that the man was young. Luke calls him a ruler. All three writers refer to the man as being rich. In that culture wealth was widely regarded as a sign of God's favor. This person has become known as the "rich young ruler" and was probably one of the officials in charge of a local synagogue, a meeting place for Jews to worship and be taught the laws of God.

Read Luke 18:18-30.

Key Words

v. 20 **commandments:** the Ten Commandments which summarize God's moral law

v. 20 **adultery:** breaking the marriage vows through sexual intercourse with a third party

v. 24 **kingdom of God:** the place or condition in which people live under

God's rule

v. 25 **camel ... eye of needle:** a Middle Eastern word picture that describes an impossibility

v. 30 **this age:** the world as we know it

today, characterized by physical death

v. 30 **age to come:** a new, coming world in which evil and death do not exist and God's rule is welcomed by all

Exploring the Passage

1. From the information we are given, how would you describe this ruler?

2. How did the ruler think he measured up to God's commandments (v. 21)?

3. Jesus listens to his answer and then adds a further requirement (v. 22). Why do you think Jesus adds such a heavy demand?

4. Jesus mentions only five of the Ten Commandments. Look them up in Exodus 20:1-17. What is especially significant about the fact that he leaves out the first and last commandment (Exodus 20:3, 17)?

5. What do you learn about the ruler from his reaction to Jesus' additional demand (v. 23)?

6. Jesus quotes a Middle Eastern saying in verse 25 that shocks his hearers. Why is it shocking?

7. How can an impossibility become a possibility (v. 27)?

8. Contrast the response of Peter to that of the rich ruler. What encouragement does Jesus give to followers who have put him first in their lives?

9. If you were to follow Jesus without reservation, what other commitments or allegiances might you have to drop?

If you have begun to follow Jesus without reservation, how has the promise of verse 30 been fulfilled already for you?

 Charting Our Course

Priorities and commitments are statements of faith. We give ourselves to what we think is most valuable. Following Jesus starts now and will continue forever. Jesus says that the value of eternal life is so great it is worth any price we must pay. Does this story give you a sense of despair or hope? Explain your answer.

4 An International Visitor Responds

Acts 8:26-39

If God is the Creator of all peoples, then it is reasonable to expect that all people experience a desire to know their Creator. How has your culture helped you to understand God? How has your culture made it difficult for you to understand God?

What were some of your first questions about the Bible?

Getting Oriented

In this reading we meet a high official in the Ethiopian government. Somehow he has learned about God and been drawn to travel a considerable distance, even into another culture, in order to respond to what he knows about God. This event occurs sometime around A.D. 33. The other person in the story is Philip, a Jewish man chosen by the twelve disciples of Jesus to supervise a food distribution program for poor widows. Philip had to leave Jerusalem because of persecution toward followers of Jesus. He was living among non-Jewish people and actively preaching about Jesus to his new neighbors.

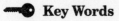 **Read** Acts 8:26-39.

Key Words

v. 26 **Jerusalem:** the key city in Israel and site of God's temple

v. 26 **Gaza:** a city in Israel about 96 kilometers (60 miles) southwest of Jerusalem

v. 27 **Ethiopia:** a large, wealthy

country in eastern Africa, called Cush in Hebrew

v. 27 **eunuch:** a castrated male employed by royalty in ancient times

v. 28 **chariot:** a horse-drawn, two-wheeled cart

v. 29 **Spirit:** in this case, the Spirit of God

v. 29 **book of Isaiah:** an Old Testament book in the Bible written by Isaiah the prophet (sixth century B.C.)

v. 37 **baptize:** refers to a religious ceremony in which a person is sprinkled or immersed in water to signify being washed clean of sin and taking on a new identity with Christ

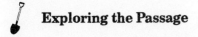 **Exploring the Passage**

1. Describe how Philip, a Jew, came to meet this Ethiopian (vv. 26-29).

2. In what ways do you see God's activity in people's lives today?

3. What seems to be the Ethiopian's attitude toward the Bible he possesses?

4. The section the Ethiopian was reading is Isaiah 53:7-8, a prophecy about the servant that God would send to earth. Why is it puzzling to him (vv. 32-34)?

5. What do you imagine Philip told the Ethiopian about Jesus' life and character?

6. What makes this "good news" (v. 35)?

7. What is the Ethiopian's response to the good news in verse 36?

8. How has Philip been a gift to the Ethiopian?

9. When Philip leaves (v. 39), why is the Ethiopian rejoicing rather than feeling sad?

10. Describe some ways God has given you opportunities to know him and the good news about Jesus.

 **Charting Our Course**

Reflecting on God's "behind-the-scenes" action in this Ethiopian's life, what are some ways God has been seeking you?

What might be a question that you need a "Philip" to answer?

5 A Military Officer Responds

Acts 10:1-48

Response to Jesus can easily become identified with one particular culture, especially if following Jesus is a practice of the majority in that culture. That's why it can be particularly helpful to meet Christians in cultures other than your own. It can bring a new perspective on Jesus.

What experiences have you had meeting followers of Jesus in other cultures?

How have those meetings influenced your thinking?

Getting Oriented

The event in this passage is a turning point in the New Testament. Up to now there were two classes of people, Jews and non-Jews (known as Gentiles). Beginning in the Old Testament, God chose one man and his descendants through whom he communicated his words to humans. These Jewish people were set apart to be a light to all other nations. Then God sent his Messiah who opened the door for other nations to relate directly to God.

In this reading an Italian military commander receives God's Spirit, and Jewish onlookers are shocked. This had never happened before. Devout Jews avoided contact with non-Jews, believing them to be unclean before God. The Jews had a strong tradition of what was clean and unclean and were forbidden to eat specific animals (see Leviticus 11). This story reveals the deep prejudice that had developed over the centuries.

 **Read** Acts 10:1-48.

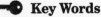 **Key Words**

v. 1 **Caesarea:** a seaport city 80 kilometers (50 miles) west of Jerusalem

v. 1 **centurion:** a Roman officer in charge of 100 soldiers

v. 1 **devout:** sincere, especially in religious matters

v. 4 **Joppa:** a seaport city about 48 kilometers (30 miles) south of Caesarea

v. 6 **tanner:** a person who prepares animal skins for use as leather

v. 19 **the Spirit:** in this case, God's Spirit

v. 28 **Gentile:** anyone who is not Jewish

v. 37 **Judea:** a province in Israel that includes the city of Jerusalem

v. 37 **Galilee:** province north of Judea where Jesus spent much of his life

v. 37 **baptism:** a religious ceremony by

water to show an identification with the life, death and resurrection of Jesus

v. 37 **Nazareth:** the town in Galilee 106 kilometers (66 miles) north of Jerusalem where Jesus grew up

v. 38 **Holy Spirit:** God's Spirit

v. 43 **prophets:** people specially called by God to speak his truth

v. 45 **circumcised:** refers to a religious ceremony performed on infant males to show that they are covered by God's promises to the Jews; "circumcised believers" refers to Jews who had come to believe in Jesus

v. 46 **speaking in tongues:** the gift of being able to speak in foreign languages as a sign of being full of God's Spirit

Exploring the Passage

1. Describe what you know of Cornelius from verses 1-8.

2. Romans worshiped numerous gods including Caesar. They were the occupation forces in conquered Israel. Jews regarded Romans as pagan and unclean. Romans regarded assignment to Israel as an unwanted tour of duty. How would these differences affect Cornelius' ability to relate to Jewish people?

3. Imagine yourself to be Cornelius. How do you feel about the words of the angel?

4. What made it difficult for Peter to obey the voice he heard (vv. 9-16)?

5. What are some accepted behaviors in your culture which would be difficult for you to give up or violate?

6. What was the first step for Peter in learning to act according to the truth of his vision?

7. Look at verses 23-33. Four days have now passed since Cornelius was visited by the angel. What indications do you see that Cornelius believed the angel?

8. Peter shares a new understanding he has received. What is it (vv. 27-29)?

9. Cornelius gives Peter an invitation to speak to his guests. What are the main points of Peter's message (vv. 34-43)?

10. How does Peter emphasize that the good news is for all peoples (vv. 42-43)?

11. Describe the response to Peter's message (vv. 44-48).

12. If people do not have to become Jewish to be clean, on what basis are they acceptable to God?

Charting Our Course

Cornelius was an Italian who came to a foreign country and learned about Jesus. In what ways does his spiritual journey resemble yours?

What have you learned about how God views your culture?

6 An Outcast Woman Responds

John 4:1-30, 39-42

Jesus crossed cultural and religious boundaries in order to reach out to people. Sometimes he caused shock and disapproval.

When you were growing up, what social or racial stereotypes were you aware of?

Why do ethnic and religious divisions still plague our world?

Getting Oriented

Hatred between Jews and Samaritans was long-standing. The Samaritans were Jews who intermarried with the enemies of Israel, and consequently most Jews would not sit, eat or drink with them. They were not allowed to worship in the temple in Jerusalem, and so the Samaritans established their own worship place in the territory of Samaria. They were regarded as outcasts and unclean before God.

∽ **Read** John 4:1-30, 39-42.

Key Words

v. 4 **Samaria:** the capital city of the northern Jewish kingdom and the name of the surrounding territory lying between Jerusalem and Galilee

v. 5 **Sychar:** a city in the territory of Samaria

v. 5 **Jacob:** the son of Isaac and father

of twelve sons who became the twelve tribes or families of the nation of Israel

v. 6 **sixth hour:** 12:00 noon

v. 22 **salvation:** deliverance or rescue from danger, especially on the Day of Judgment

v. 24 **spirit:** the nonphysical, eternal

and essential character of a person
v. 25 **Messiah:** a Hebrew title meaning "the chosen one"

v. 42 **Savior:** one who frees, saves from danger

Exploring the Passage

1. In verse 8 Jesus asks the Samaritan woman for a drink of water. Why does this simple request surprise her?

2. What are some present-day racial, religious or sexual barriers that keep people segregated?

3. In verses 10-15 Jesus and the woman seem to be talking at two different levels. Describe the difference.

4. How does Jesus describe God's attitude toward this outcast woman (vv. 10, 13)?

5. In verse 16 the discussion turns a corner. What do we learn about this woman in verses 16-18?

6. How might this explain why she was at the well alone and in the heat of the day?

What are some other ways people seek to fill the longings in their lives?

7. The woman changes the subject in verses 19-20 and opens the door to a long-standing controversy. How does Jesus' answer avoid an ethnic standoff?

8. This woman, though an outcast, reveals some spiritual understanding in verse 25. What caused her to become convinced that Jesus was the Messiah?

9. How does she respond to this new understanding Jesus gives her in verses 28-30?

10. How does this woman's experience affect her society?

What message does Jesus communicate by staying there for two days?

 **Charting Our Course**

Ethnic and religious traditions can prevent people from coming to know God, as can feelings of unworthiness. How does it make you feel to know that Jesus knows everything about you, yet is not put off by that?

Describe any "thirst" that you have at this time.

The Final Word: Passport to Life

In section four, we explored the stories of five people who responded to God's invitation to embrace Jesus—God's chosen one who brings eternal life and forgiveness of sins to all who put their trust in him. You may also be ready to move from being a spectator to being a participant and begin a personal relationship with Jesus.

John 1:12 says, "to all who received him, to those who believed in his name, he [Jesus] gave the right to become children of God." This relationship begins when we both *believe something* and *receive someone.* We believe that Jesus is God's "sent one" to bring God's words to us and to die for our sins, and we receive Jesus as our Shepherd and Lord. Would you like to do this now? The following is a prayer you could speak to God to express your desire.

> Loving God who is seeking me, I want to know you personally as my heavenly Father. I have come to see in Jesus the truth of who you are. In that truth I recognize my failure to love and trust you with all of my heart and mind. I now turn from my independence and welcome you as my Lord. Jesus, thank you for dying for my sin and offering me forgiveness and a new life that will never end. Please come into my life and fill me with your Holy Spirit. As your grateful child, I am prepared to serve you with all my heart, mind and will. Amen [may it be so].

If you have begun a personal relationship with God by committing yourself to follow Jesus, then the Bible has become your passport to eternal life. Welcome to God's worldwide family!

Continuing in Bible Study

Like any relationship with a human being, your relationship with God must be carefully nurtured by regular communication. When you committed yourself to Jesus as your Savior and Lord, he sent his Holy Spirit into your heart to be your Counselor, Teacher and Helper. The Holy Spirit will help you understand the Bible, give you direction from God and make you more like Jesus.

You may use the method of Bible study in this guide, asking and answering questions about the Bible passage, to listen to God as you read the Bible. Each time you read the Bible, begin by asking for the Holy Spirit's help in understanding and applying God's Word. Then you may ask yourself some of these questions:

☐ What does this passage show me about a sin I should confess and turn from or an error to avoid?

☐ Is there an example that I should follow or a promise I should claim?

☐ What does this passage teach me about God the Father, Son or Holy Spirit?

☐ What does this passage show me about myself?

After you have listened to God's voice through the Bible, then respond to him in prayers of praise for his goodness and love, prayers of thanks for blessings he has given you and prayers asking his help for yourself or others. Jesus taught us that God cares about every detail of our lives.

God's Family

Developing a strong relationship with God's family is also important for growing in your life in God. Ask God to lead you to a church that will help you learn more about trusting him.

It is important to understand that eternal life is not a carefree life in which God gives us everything we ask for. In fact, Paul strengthened new churches by telling them, "We must go through many hardships to enter the kingdom of God" (Acts 14:22). But although he doesn't promise us an easy life, God does promise us his presence and help.

We must also remember that eternal life is a free gift that cannot be earned by anything we do. Bible study, prayer, participation in Christian fellowship and doing good things all strengthen our relationship with God; they do not earn us our place in God's family.

It is because we belong to God that we do these things.

Although God doesn't always give us what we want, he does promise a full life (John 10:10) of meaning and purpose, joy, peace and love, and rich relationships. Jesus invites us to dine with him—a picture of intimate fellowship: "Here I am! I stand at the door and knock. If anyone hears my voice and opens the door, I will come in and eat with him and he with me" (Revelation 3:20). This verse invites every person to a friendship deeper and stronger than any human friendship—a friendship that extends beyond death into life with God for all eternity.

Suggestions for Leaders
Katie Rawson

Recently I was asked at the last minute to lead a Bible discussion on the claims of Jesus Christ. I had just a little while to read through the text and study guide before the group meeting started. Fortunately, I was very familiar with the passage and the study guide made the purposes of the study clear. The group was perceptive and talkative, and the discussion went well.

Afterward I chatted with a newcomer from China. Liyan had attended Bible studies for three years elsewhere and had just moved to our area. When she found out that I was researching how to best share the Christian faith with East Asian students, one question after another began to tumble out of her mouth. Before the evening was over, Liyan had decided to become a follower of Jesus Christ!

Such joyful experiences occasionally happen to leaders of studies designed for people investigating the Bible for the first time. We "reap a harvest" that others have sown and watered. But patient preparation of the soil through group-building and faithful planting of the seed through Bible discussions is how investigative group leaders spend most of their time. How best can we prepare the soil, plant, water and reap through group studies?

The material in *Passport to the Bible* will be helpful for seekers from almost any country. And it can be useful to Christians desiring an overview of the Bible's major themes. If your group contains mostly Christians, you may need to add some application or reflection questions appropriate for them.

Leading Investigative Groups
Leading a group designed for seekers rather than for followers of Jesus requires prayer, persistence and sensitivity. But the rewards can be very great. It is wise to share the responsibility with a coleader who can pray, care for people individually and take a turn at leading when needed. Do not allow the group to become overloaded with believers, however. They could intimidate the seekers you want to serve.

In order to orient group members to the Bible, walk them through the Bible overview material, "The Big Picture," before you begin the studies. Ask people to commit to one set of six studies at a time. If the first series goes well, they will want to continue.

How do you prepare the soil? Most people with spiritual longings today are looking for relationships and experience as well as knowledge. Therefore it is essential to make the group more than a weekly intellectual discussion. Try to build community through common meals, activities, get-acquainted exercises and social times before or after the meeting. (See the *Small Group Leaders' Handbook* and the *Big Book on Small Groups* [InterVarsity Press] for more help.)

Investigative group members need both the security of being cared for and the freedom to seek spiritual truth at their own pace. So it is crucial not to pressure people to commit to Jesus when they aren't ready. It is also crucial to be open to any question or response they may have.

People from certain cultures may give the answer they believe the leader wants, in order not to offend, rather than saying what they really think. Strive to develop real friendships so that people will feel free to be honest in the group meeting. Phoning or having coffee with group members between meetings to find out how they are doing helps to build trust. By making the group a pressure-free but caring place, you provide the atmosphere needed to facilitate the decision to follow Jesus. When the time comes to call an individual to commitment, the Holy Spirit will make that clear to you.

In the past, leaders of investigative studies were often advised to omit prayer in order not to offend the seekers present. This still may be advisable with certain groups (our informal prayers might seem irreverent to Muslims, for example). However, most people today want a practical faith and an experience of God. Seeing answers to prayer and experiencing Christian worship is a part of coming to believe in God for many. So you might consider including a brief worship time at the beginning and prayer for the needs of group members at the end of the discussion. And encourage seekers to act on what they are learning. Jesus tells us in John 7:17 that God reveals the truth to those who obey his will.

Preparing the Study

1. As you study the passage, ask God to help you understand and apply it to your own life. Pray that group members will be open to the Holy Spirit as you discuss the text.

2. Be prepared to answer the introductory question with personal feelings or examples. The group will be only as open as you are.

3. Read and reread the text to become familiar with it. This guide is based on the New International Version (NIV), so you will want to do most of your reading in this translation.

4. Think through each question in the study carefully and write out your responses. The act of writing helps us clarify our thoughts. Keep in mind the length of time you have for the study. Highlight those questions that most clearly accomplish the purpose of the study as stated in the Leader's Notes. If your group is running short on time, be sure to ask these questions; others can be omitted.

5. Reflect carefully on the final question(s) under "Charting Our Course." Be willing to share how they apply to your own life, as you encourage others to do the same.

Leading the Discussion

1. Be sure everyone in the group has a copy of the guide and the text in the NIV translation. Try to make sure that everyone is seated in a circle so they can see everyone else well and so that you can see everyone's face. Facial expressions will sometimes give you a clue as to how people are reacting, even if they say nothing.

2. At the first meeting, explain that the studies are meant to be discussions not lectures. Read through the guidelines for group studies found at the end of the introductory article, "Exploring the Bible," and explain that these are the ground rules for the discussions. If group members have not read the introduction to the guide, then share some of the introductory material and the "seekers' prayer" with them.

3. Begin the study on time, opening with prayer if it's appropriate for your group.

4. The study's introduction and introductory question(s) are designed to catch the attention of group members, break the ice and draw everyone into the discussion. Be sure to ask the question before the text is read so that no one's answers are colored by the biblical material.

5. *Passport to the Bible* includes a set of key terms at the beginning of each study, especially biblical and theological phrases that may be unfamiliar to those who have not read much of the Bible. Discuss any key terms or biblical words which your group might not understand.

6. To begin, have one member read the passage aloud. Or if the text contains dialogue, various members may take parts and role play the passage. If several people have limited English comprehension, ask the group to also read the text silently and identify any unfamiliar words.

7. The questions are designed to be used just as they are written. You may read them directly from the guide or put them in your own words. If a question has already been answered, skip it and go on. If someone asks a question directly related to the text, have the group try to answer it. Unrelated questions, unless they can be answered quickly, should be recorded and addressed later.

8. In an investigative study it is important to take the questions group members raise seriously, so a way must be found to address them. You may have to research the question and report the following week—or even plan a later Bible study to cover it. Questions may also be answered during the informal social time which follows many group meetings.

9. Don't answer your own questions! Rephrase them until they are clearly understood. When a leader provides the "right" answers, group members lose interest quickly.

10. Don't be afraid of silence. People may need time to think before answering.

11. Most of the questions should have more than one answer. Ask, "What do others think?" Continue until several replies have been given.

12. Acknowledge all contributions and affirm whenever possible. Never reject a response. If an answer is clearly incorrect, ask "Which verse led you to that conclusion?" or "What do others think?" Encourage members to look for answers in the text being studied.

13. When members start interacting with each other and not simply addressing every comment to you, then healthy discussion is occurring. There may be a "warm-up" period before this happens.

14. Get the discussion started with your own responses to the question(s) under "Charting Your Course," even though others may not be ready to speak up. Some group members may prefer to simply think about the question. If appropriate, encourage group members to write down their responses privately.

15. Before closing you may want to ask if there are any questions. Sometimes there are still significant questions in a group member's mind. If a question can't be handled in a couple of minutes, you might say, "Let's close, and then those who are interested can continue discussing this question."

16. End on time. After the group meeting is over, spend some time privately in prayer, asking God to protect the seed of his Word which has been planted in the hearts of group members.

17. If anyone in the group has indicated readiness to commit to following Jesus, follow up with that person during the next week. A prayer for committing to Jesus may be found in the section entitled "The Final Word."

Working with Crosscultural Groups

Groups made up of people from more than one country present special challenges. How does one facilitate a discussion among people with different views of the world and different learning styles? One question that needs to be asked at the outset is, "Would some, or all, members of this group be more comfortable in same-sex rather than mixed groups?" Sometimes international women are hesitant to speak in groups containing men, especially their husbands. And in some cultures, mixed gender groups are not appropriate.

You will also have the challenge of bringing together people with varied worldviews. Awareness of cultural differences may be built by sharing information about the biblical cultures when appropriate. Ask questions such as "How would most people from your country interpret (or react to) this verse?"

People from sub-Saharan Africa and certain tribal groups usually resonate with the biblical kinship cultures discussed in the introductory article "Exploring the Bible." East and some Southeast Asians have their roots in peasant cultures, and Westerners usually resonate with urban culture types. As group members learn more about each other's backgrounds and about the biblical message, a "group culture" with shared understandings may develop. While this is happening, you may need to periodically remind the group of the ground rules for the discussions.

The people in your group may also have diverse learning styles. To communicate well, try using all the senses. Include short clips from videos on the life of Jesus in some of your studies on Jesus. Suggest that people highlight key words or ideas on their copies of the text, using colored pens. Use a flip chart for recording the group's answers to certain questions. Bring in books with paintings of the biblical scenes or photographs of biblical movies. Play a brief segment of a CD which brings out a theme in the text. And, if it is appropriate for your group, have members role-play passages with dialogue or action. (Each of these suggestions is appropriate for some cultural groups but not for others. If you are not sure, ask a group member in advance what will work.)

The religious background of your group members will also be a factor. Buddhists may not understand the meaning of sin or the concept of forgiveness. Hindus will be affronted by the concept of sacrifice. Muslims insist (as do Jews) that God is one and will struggle with Jesus' claim to be the Son of God as well as with the idea of the Trinity.

There are points of common ground from which you can begin discussion. Muslims respect the Old Testament prophets and revere Jesus as a messenger from God. Buddhists admire examples of self-giving and compassion for those who suffer. Hindus will be more drawn to the conceptual language of John's writings than to the descriptive style of Mark or Luke.

Asians tend to be pictorial thinkers and are drawn to both the parables and the personal encounters of Jesus. Hindus, being more abstract thinkers, will need to grasp the character of the God of the Bible. Buddhists and Hindus will not appreciate the problem of sin until they know something of the character of God. Muslims insist that God is holy, but in reality they hope in his mercy and their own merit. They also fail to see the problem sin creates. In fact, the work of Jesus as God's remedy for the problem of sin will make little sense to internationals and postmodern Americans. First they need a clear understanding of who God is and the nature of the human condition. (For this reason, use the first two sets of studies before moving on to the others.)

These tendencies obviously depend on the depth of religious knowledge and commitment of the individuals. And postmodernism is affecting and changing us all.

If your group has primarily people from one cultural background or one region of the world, you may be able to adapt the style of your meetings to one which is especially comfortable for them. East Asians are used to lectures, so you may want to do a little more teaching when leading them than when leading Americans. But take cultural adaptation only so far. We use the inductive Bible study method in this guide because we want your group members to learn the method as well as the content of the biblical texts. A person who becomes a follower of Jesus through using these studies should already know how to feed himself or herself by asking questions of the Bible. Since many international students become Christians and then return home quickly, it will be very helpful if they already know how to study Scripture for personal growth.

Understanding the Audience

It is difficult to become an expert on many different cultures. For most of us it is a challenge to learn one new culture well! But I have found a certain set of questions helpful as I try to understand other people more deeply. They are questions that help us share God's good news effectively in any culture. These are not questions you ask the members of your group, but questions you ask yourself *about* them in order to understand them better.

□ *Are my words and actions building or undermining trust with this individual?* Trust is an essential ingredient in any relationship.

□ *What is my friend's worldview?* A worldview is a person's basic assumptions about reality. Worldviews are often unconscious; they include beliefs, feelings and values. It is especially important for us to understand an individual's beliefs about God and humankind.

□ *What false assumptions may be preventing my friend from understanding and responding to the gospel?* Lies that people believe about God, themselves and other aspects of reality may hinder them from coming to faith. One such lie is, "I'm not good enough to become a Christian. I need to wait until I've cleaned myself up." In 2 Corinthians 10:3-5, Paul calls such lies "strongholds." When the Holy Spirit reveals strongholds to us, we can pray against them and prayerfully share opposite truths with our friends.

□ *What is God already doing in this person's life?* Since Jesus did only what he saw the Father doing (John 5:19), it makes sense for us to try to discern what God is doing in a person's life so we can cooperate with him!

□ *What is "good news" to this person or group? What aspect of the character of God or of the gospel message directly meets their need?* Hearing an individual's life story will often help in answering this question.

Adapting the Studies for English-Language Learners
With a little work these studies may be adapted for students at an intermediate level of English-language learning. Your first task is to choose an easier translation and make copies of the text in it. The *New International Readers' Version, Today's English (Good News)* or *Contemporary English Version* are all possible. I prefer *Good News* because of the availability of bilingual Bibles in this version. You should also locate Bibles in the languages of group members. Next, read through the questions and revise any that depend on the NIV wording or use vocabulary that is too difficult. Choose one or two questions to omit, since some of your group time may be spent discussing words or phrases. Focus on questions which fulfill the purpose of the study. Circle all difficult words in the text so that you can define them during the group meeting.

In the meeting itself, allow the group time to read the text silently in English and in their languages, looking up words when needed. Discuss all the terms you think may be difficult; students are sometimes embarrassed to take group time by admitting they don't know a certain word. Pronounce any difficult words and names yourself and then give everyone a chance to read aloud. Most will enjoy the English practice. Keep a keen eye out for expressions of confusion. Use a flip chart to write down difficult words introduced in the discussion and to summarize group findings. And take time for frequent questions and answers during the meeting.

Building a Prayer Foundation
In 1 Corinthians 3:7 Paul reminds us that God is the one who makes things grow. All of our preparing of the soil, planting and watering is useless if God's Spirit is not at work. Paul goes on to say that we dare not build on any foundation other than Jesus Christ. How do we make sure we are building on the foundation of Christ? Through prayer. It is wise to recruit a group of intercessors who will pray daily for you and the group members.

Even though it has only been a month since Liyan invited the Lord into her life, she is already reaching out to other Chinese in the group. The wonderful thing about God's harvests is that they multiply! May God grant you wisdom, discernment and grace as you work in his field through leading these studies.

Leader's Notes

The Big Picture

To give group members an overview of the Bible, you may want to spend your first session together discussing the material in "The Big Picture." Have group members refer to the "Bible at a Glance" chart (p. 11) as you go through the survey material. Your Bible may contain additional visual helps which would aid group members. *The Bible Visual Resource Book* (Regal) contains reproducible maps, charts, time lines and graphics which are excellent orientation materials for group or individual Bible study. You might want to make a poster outlining or diagramming the five periods of biblical history presented in the overview. Seeing this material graphically could help group members get the "big picture" better. It would also be helpful to read and briefly discuss some of the verses referred to in this section.

PART ONE: Meeting God
Study 1. The God of Mystery. Genesis 1:1—2:3.

Purpose: To gain understanding of God by looking at God the Creator.

Introduction. Give some time for people to think about their childhood before encouraging them to speak. For those who are not free to speak of themselves, ask them about their culture's thinking.

Getting Oriented. Reinforce the place that Genesis has in the history of Western civilization. Point out that all of the concern for worldwide human rights as well as our notions about democracy stem from these first three chapters. Invite people to identify any terms they don't understand.

Question 1. Verse 1 establishes a first cause and names it God. He is creative, very powerful, much more intelligent than humans.

Question 2. From nothing he speaks things into existence. His word is the agent of creation.

Question 3. There is a pattern of days and of certain phrases: let there be ... there was ... God saw ... it was good.

Question 4. Notice day/night, sky/land, land/seas.

Question 5. Notice solar system, fish, birds, animals, humans.

Question 6. They are "very good," "in God's image," given instructions and given authority. Be sensitive to people in your group who may worship idols as you ask this question.

Question 7. The range of possibilities includes having the capacity to choose, form relationships, love, create, and experience joy or satisfaction.

Question 8. To fill and increase, to rule and care for—in other words, to cooperate with God by acting as a caretaker of his creation.

Question 9. It establishes rhythm and boundaries to life. There is work and rest. It gives us the opportunity to demonstrate that we were made like God.

Question 10. It establishes the value and meaning of all life. It gives purpose and direction to work. It honors diversity. It answers many *why* questions.

Charting Our Course. See the book *The Universe Next Door* to understand the implications of alternative answers to the question of origins. If there was no Creator, then life is the result of chance and cannot have any assigned significance. If there is a Creator, but the Creator is not personal, then there can be no relationship between humans and God, and we are truly alone.

Study 2. The God Who Is Near. Psalm 139.

Purpose: Through the meditations of David, we come face to face with a God who is intimate and aware of our every thought and breath.

Getting Oriented. Create a nonthreatening atmosphere in which people can freely express their ideas even if they do not believe there is a God.

Question 1. God seeks intimate understanding of us no matter what we are doing, even when we sleep. He knows what we think even before we speak. He has his hands around us.

Question 2. We are not incidental to God, not ignored, not blips on a radar screen, not a bother, not unimportant. God takes the initiative in relationship with us.

Question 3. Actions, thoughts, speech and intentions.

Question 4. I can't go anywhere, not into hell, not east, not west, not into darkness, where God is not present.

Question 6. He created us. He has a plan for us. We are not an aimless cork bobbing in the sea.

Question 8. God is not someone to fear but rather to embrace. He is personal, intimate, caring and knowing.

Question 9. (1) You are so great and therefore should eliminate all who hate you. (2) Test me to make sure I do not offend you in any way. Be my leader.

Study 3. God *Is* Great. Isaiah 40:9-31.

Purpose: To see God's greatness in relation to life on earth and to realize that he is still personal and approachable—our only solid basis for hope.

Getting Oriented. Our aspirations mark us and mock us, for no matter how noble our aims, the truth is that grass withers, flowers fall and we die. Only God is permanent. This can be a cause for despair or a motivation to connect with the ever-living God.

Question 1. "Sovereign," "shepherd," "creator," "sits over the earth," "life in his hands." Note how many are pictures of power.

Question 2. The shepherd image (v. 11) may strike some as out of place. So might the picture of God giving strength (vv. 29-31).

Question 3. The same arm that rules and judges also gathers up lambs.

Question 5. We can partly understand God by analogies, but God is always bigger and outside our analogies.

Questions 6-7. An idol is anything we worship or become enslaved to. Nations can make idols of political institutions, economic prosperity and military might. Individuals can idolize relationships or money.

Question 9. We have a solid basis for hope. Our hope is in the character of God who is both sovereign and gentle shepherd.

Study 4. God's Promises. Deuteronomy 5:1-21, 28; 6:1-9.

Purpose: To understand the standards of God as reflections of his character.

Getting Oriented. The laws we most respect are those we understand and agree are good for our welfare or for the greater society. This study focuses on gaining a greater appreciation and understanding of God's laws.

Question 2. The first four laws deal with our relationship to God. The fifth law deals with parents. Laws 6-10 deal with community life.

Question 3. He is jealous for our allegiance. He takes responsibility for our welfare. His love is greater than his hatred. He is jealous about his name. He wants one day in seven.

Question 4. He implies that they belong to him by virtue of his acts for them.

Question 5. Our worship by its intensity, or lack of it, shows who we give our allegiance to.

Question 6. If these laws are followed, relationships are enhanced and community is strengthened. If these laws are neglected, relationships are damaged and community is fragmented.

Question 8. These laws are established as part of a vital relationship with God. To break one is to break trust and to dishonor God.

Question 10. The right reason comes out of personal relationship, wanting to please someone we care for.

Charting Our Course. The laws don't move to our hearts unless they are part of a relationship in which covenant-keeping is based on honor, respect and love.

Study 5. God's Standards. Luke 10:25-37.

Purpose: To see clearly the absolute standard of God that renders all humans guilty of missing the mark.

Question 3. He gives an outstanding summary of the heart of the law.

Obedience is synonymous with love. If he is correct, then who is blameless?
No one.

Question 4. The law expert shows his true nature: he quibbles over the
easiest part and avoids what is most difficult.

Question 5. Jesus tells a story that exposes the importance of heart
attitudes over outward acts.

Question 6. The choice of a Samaritan as the hero.

Question 8. The true neighbor is not the priest or the law expert, but a
despised person regarded as unclean because of his ethnicity. The first two
men followed the letter of the law, but the Samaritan obeyed from the
heart.

Question 9. Love comes from the heart, and its fruit is compassion.

Question 10. God's standards are based on heart attitudes rather than
external perfection.

Study 6. The God Who Wants Us to Seek Him. Acts 17:16-32.
Purpose: To see God as one who is eager for relationship with humans.

Question 3. They had many altars and images of gods.

Question 4. Compare verse 16 with verses 24-25. The Creator God cannot
be likened to any object or confined to a shrine. He is one God, over all,
and he deserves the worship of all. (Encourage group members to share
the concept of God their background taught.)

Question 5. He wants people to seek him and enjoy relationship with him.

Question 6. He is not far away. In him (whether we know it or not) we
live and move and have our being.

Question 7. *Repentance* means that we agree with God's assessment of
us, apologize to him, stop following our own ideas and begin following his
way.

Charting Our Course. This passage shows us that God actually wants
us to look for him and find him. It also shows that repentance is very
important—and necessary in establishing contact with God.

PART TWO: Who Am I?
Study 1. Made for Relationship. Genesis 2:4-25.
Purpose: To recognize that human beings were made to have right relationships with God and with each other, and to see that life's problems
stem from the lack of these right relationships.

Read. It can be helpful to give the group time to read the passage to
themselves silently, then discuss the words they are unfamiliar with, and
finally to read the passage aloud. This takes a little extra time, but it helps
the group to be ready to enter into discussion.

General Note. If anyone asks about the repetition of the creation story
in the early chapters of Genesis, tell them that all of chapter 1 and the

beginning of chapter 2 in Genesis are basically a quick overview of how God created the universe. Most of chapter 2, however, offers us a more detailed look at how God created the first man and woman.

Question 2. God's actions show the deep and personal nature of his love for the man and the woman.

Question 3. Don't spend too long on this question. Make it clear that you will look in depth at these verses shortly. For now, try to get a basic impression from this passage: man was formed directly by God (v. 7); he was put in the Garden to take care of it (v. 15); he was told what to eat and what not to eat (vv. 16-17); and it was not good for him to be alone (v. 18).

Question 4. Most people consider work as a burden or a duty. It does not usually enter into our ideas of paradise or utopia.

Question 5. It may help to ask people to consider the question: Which parents are more loving—the ones who give their child everything he or she wants, or the ones who sometimes say no to their child's requests?

Question 6. It might seem that the man's every need had been met, but his need for companionship had not yet been fulfilled.

Question 7. The woman was made from the man and for the man, and God himself brought her to the man. The intimacy of the connection that God intended between them is evident from the very beginning; God's tender concern for the needs of the man and the woman can be seen in his actions here.

Question 8. God is interested in our emotional needs, even so "small" a thing as our loneliness, and went to great lengths to provide just the right solution for the man. He will similarly provide what is best for each of us.

Study 2. What Went Wrong? Genesis 3.

Purpose: To understand what caused broken relationships among people and between people and God.

Getting Oriented. Don't let this become a big discussion of possible reasons for pain in the world. Get people started thinking about the topic, and then move quickly into the Bible study.

Question 1. The serpent is crafty, and in his speech he questions God. He is challenging God's authority, and also trying to damage the relationship of love and trust between God and the humans.

Question 2. Notice that the woman has exaggerated God's command, adding "you must not touch it" (although this is less of an exaggeration than what the serpent said in v. 1).

Question 3. The woman seems to view God's command as a restriction more than a safeguard. If it seems appropriate, you might also ask, "What are some ways humans make God more restrictive than he intends to be?"

Question 4. Satan has offered the woman a "shortcut" to deity, power,

wisdom: eat the fruit and be like God. In fact, he has also called God a liar
(v. 4) and has represented him as trying to keep some good thing from the
man and the woman (v. 5).

Question 5. The woman wants an easy path to power, and she wants
knowledge. She also doubts God. If the woman truly thought she would
die, she would not have eaten the fruit. Her actions show that she doubted
God.

Question 6. The element of fear has entered into all these relationships.
Also, there is the element of guilt—and of trying to pass the blame off on
others. (Notice that the man was there with the woman when all this
happened [v. 6].)

Question 7. Allow time for group members to think about their own
real-life experiences. Don't let this become a distraction from the Bible
study, but ask several to share with the group. If people seem intimidated
by this question, point out that they don't need to give details about the
incident but just talk about the relationship.

You might also ask, "What could be said to have died in that relationship?" (Among the relationships that died were those between humans
and God, humans and nature, man and woman, woman and child, humans
and work.)

Question 8. They questioned God's honesty and goodness. They tried to
meet their needs in their own way, by their own strength—and in so doing,
they ended up hurting themselves, each other and their relationships
(with God and with one another).

Question 9. Consider why God did what he did. God did not want the man
and the woman to be trapped forever in this (now) sinful world. He sent
them away so that they would not have to live forever on this fallen planet.

Question 10. Don't make too much of this as an allusion to Christ, but
you can mention it, if it is appropriate to your group. The main point is
that God will provide a solution to this problem that the man and the
woman have created.

Charting Our Course. Be sure that people see the love and goodness of
God. Even in the face of open doubt and rebellion, God continued to protect
the humans and to make a way for them once again to have a relationship
with him.

Study 3. What Is the Point of Life? Ecclesiastes 1:12—2:26.

Purpose: To see that whether we pursue meaning through pleasure or
performance, we will ultimately find meaning only in having a right
relationship with God.

General Note. This is a long passage. Don't get bogged down; keep things
moving. You might want to divide the passage into four parts: 1:12-18;
2:1-10; 2:11-16; 2:17-26. Read one section, then discuss it before moving

on to read the next section.

Question 2. Notice specific things Solomon mentions doing. What Solomon describes here is basically hedonism: If it feels good, do it.

Question 3. Remember that as king, he would have all the wealth and power that goes with such a position. This wealth and power would give him the opportunity to do as he pleased. Also note that when Solomon speaks of seeking "wisdom" (v. 3), he may be referring to his search for the meaning and purpose of life: What is the wise way to live?

Question 4. Although he saw that wisdom (good sense, good judgment) is better than folly, he eventually realized that both the wise man and the fool will die and be forgotten. Their end is the same.

Question 5. No matter how hard you work or how much you save and store up, you must leave it all to those who come after you.

Question 7. Everything comes from God. Therefore, people should trust him and find satisfaction in the simple tasks of life.

Question 8. Have everyone read these verses for themselves—the very last verses in Ecclesiastes. Then allow for more than one person to answer this question.

Charting Our Course. Some may not feel comfortable answering these questions aloud. You may want to allow a time of silent reflection instead. You will need to gauge the comfort level of your group.

Study 4. Your Place in God's Family. Luke 15:11-32.

Purpose: To understand God's attitude toward us when we do wrong: he longs to forgive us and to have an honest and loving relationship with us.

General Note. In discussing the concept of sin, it is often helpful to describe it in terms of selfishness and self-centeredness. Many people who don't consider themselves sinful will admit to being selfish. Whether we are more of a rebel or a self-righteous person, we all need the love and forgiveness of our heavenly Father to make things right in our lives.

Getting Oriented. An alternate opening question could be, "Which phrase best describes you: 'I do my own thing' or 'I do what I'm told'?" (An explanation of these phrases may be necessary.)

Question 1. The son does not seem at all interested in his relationship with his father. He wants his share of the estate, and even asks for it before his father's death (the normal time for receiving it).

Question 2. The father is not weak or foolish, but loving, wise and practical. He knows that any son who would make such a bold request does not understand the deep love of the father for him.

Question 4. The key moment comes when he longs to eat the pigs' food (v. 17). Note the phrase, "He came to his senses."

Question 5. Consider not only changed circumstances, but also changed attitudes. He left cocky, self-assured and indifferent to his father's love. He returned humbled, grateful and willing to work as a hired man.

Question 6. The father recognized that for the son to come home was in itself an admission of failure, guilt, remorse and need. He did not belittle his son's past foolish behavior and failure but sought instead to demonstrate his deep love.

Questions 7-8. Some may see the older brother as "the good son" and may find the father's actions puzzling. Try to help them see that the older brother was not motivated by love and did not understand or care about the father's love. His pettiness and bitterness reveal what motivated his behavior. Both brothers at first thought only of themselves and their own needs and advantage. Only the younger brother changed.

Question 9. Notice the father's gentle reminder of the truth (v. 31) and his attempt to help the older brother think of more than his own needs. The father was just as patient and forgiving with the older son's act of rebellion and selfishness as he had been with that of the younger son at the start of the parable.

Charting Our Course. These two brothers typify all of us. Remind the group of their answers to the opening question as a demonstration of that fact. If people are uncomfortable discussing this aloud, just let them think about it. Pray for good one-on-one conversations afterward.

Study 5. Where Does Evil Come From? Mark 7:1-23.

Purpose: To understand that the evil in this world comes from our own sinful human natures.

Introduction. Keep the discussion of countries' serious problems brief. Don't let it get out of hand and use up the study time.

Question 1. The Pharisees and the teachers of the law were very careful to follow certain rules of cleanliness, washing themselves in particular ways. These practices were more symbols and rituals than an actual soap-and-water cleansing. They were, in fact, not part of the Law which God gave through Moses, but were added later as interpretations and applications of that Law. Jesus' disciples were not keeping these "traditions of the elders" (v. 3)—in other words, human laws. This led the Pharisees and the teachers of the law to view Jesus' disciples as less spiritual, less godly, less serious in their religious endeavors.

Question 2. The Pharisees and teachers of the law were questioning Jesus over the failure of his disciples to keep a *human interpretation* of the Bible's dietary laws, yet these religious leaders had themselves failed to keep the clear *command of God* to honor their parents. Don't let discussion run too far ahead of you here; simply set the tone for the verses that follow.

Question 4. Jesus sees uncleanness as coming from within the human heart, not as entering from without.

It is probably best not to mention the following unless it comes up, but Jesus' view of the source of sin and evil is very different from that of many religions (such as, Buddhism or Hinduism) which teach that humans are pure beings who have been corrupted by an impure world.

It can help sometimes to define sin or impurity as "selfishness." Many people will deny that they are "sinners" (which they see as some extreme form of evil), but most will recognize their own selfishness. You can address this matter now or leave it until the conclusion of the study, depending upon what is more appropriate to the course of the discussion.

Question 6. In Jesus' description of the human problem, no person or ethnic group is any better or worse than any other.

Question 7. Answers will vary—for example, Buddhist vegetarianism, prayer and fasting; Hindu vegetarianism, yoga and meditation; Muslim fasting, alms giving, five-times daily prayer and pilgrimages to Mecca; Christian church attendance, Bible reading and prayer; New Age meditation, vegetarianism, and "random acts of kindness and senseless acts of beauty."

Question 9. The responses of the group members will vary, but note that only solutions that address human *motives* and not merely human *behavior* will have any lasting impact.

Charting Our Course. See the Leader's Notes for question 4 regarding sin and selfishness. Even if people do not agree with Jesus' teaching here, they should at least understand what he has said and meant in this passage. Be sure that the connection between selfishness and sin is made and understood.

Study 6. Turning from Sorrow to Joy. Psalm 32.

Purpose: To discover that relationship with God is broken by our sin but repair is readily available because, when we admit to what we have done, God willingly forgives.

Introduction. If no one feels free to talk about personal family matters, broaden the question to apply to relationships in general.

Question 3. Things changed when he took responsibility for his actions and confessed them.

Question 5. "Don't delay." "Don't wait to be coerced." Living in the truth about ourselves is ultimate safety because it brings us into relationship with God, and then he can instruct, counsel and protect us.

Question 7. God's unfailing love is upon all who live in a trust relationship with him. We can use our understanding to seek God and to live in truth. We have enough understanding to move toward God and do not need to wait.

Question 8. We can use our understanding to seek God and to live in truth. We have enough understanding to move toward God; we do not need to wait to be coerced.

PART THREE: Good News!
Study 1. Good News for the World. Luke 2:1-20.
Purpose: To discover that Jesus' birth is utterly unique.
General note. God sees Jesus' birth as good news of great joy for all people. This message is so important that God sent his angels to proclaim it. It's so powerful God allowed lowly shepherds to tell others. It's so secure that his birth could take place in a humble stable. It's so wonderful that it causes people and angels to be joyful and give praise to God.
Introduction. Events surrounding our birth may play a role in influencing how we see ourselves and how others view us: our class or caste, whether we are poor or rich, whether it's a time of war or peace, even the size of our family. Help people to share briefly. Some may never have thought about their own birth.
Question 1. The Roman government had the power to make all residents, no matter where they lived and worked, return to their town of birth for the census. This would disrupt everyone's life.
Question 2. Mary is pregnant and must travel a great distance (no cars or buses!). This is her first experience giving birth and she is taken away from her family, her friends, midwives and support group. And she's not even married yet! From the text it appears she had no help with the birth (*she* wrapped him in cloths and placed him in the manger).
Question 3. The answers to this may vary depending on the culture or experiences of the participants. Generally shepherds have low status.
Question 5. The angel says not to be afraid, that it's good news, it's for all people (which includes them), the savior (one who saves) is born to them, he is the Christ (the chosen one), and he is the Lord (the owner, the master). He also tells them they will find a baby (babies are not very frightening).
Question 6. If God wanted to tell such wonderful news to lowly shepherds, then he must surely want us to know as well! God is interested in everyone. Note that God used angels to announce it to the shepherds but then used shepherds to announce it to the rest of the people.
Question 7. This is a "what do you suppose" kind of question, so answers may vary. Perhaps they were excited that they had been given the good news so wanted to share it with others. Perhaps they saw how important this news was for everyone to hear. They were certainly impressed with the fact that God was doing something very important, yet God did it in a very humble way and they could have a part.
Question 8. A number of things could be listed: the amazing things the angels said about Jesus (vv. 10-14); the contrasts in messengers—angels appearing in heaven and earthly shepherds spreading the word; contrasts in the context—the Lord being born under terrible conditions (harsh Roman occupying government, unclean stable, unmarried mother, so simple and poor).

Charting Our Course. God is concerned about the lowliest and most difficult situations. God wants *all people* to know his good news of great joy (Jesus). Jesus has been born for each of us (v. 11). God wants us to know that Jesus is Christ and Lord. He wants us to experience his peace and favor (v. 14) and to tell others about it.

Study 2. Good News for Sinners. Mark 2:1-17.
Purpose: To discover that Jesus' authority goes beyond healing physical sickness to healing spiritual sickness.

Introduction. Because this may be such a personal question, people may just think about it silently, and that is fine. Group members may realize that they have no idea how to get rid of heavy loads; this Bible study will help them discover how.

Question 1. "Getting Oriented" gives a brief summary of Mark 1. The people have heard all that Jesus has been doing, and when they hear that Jesus has come home, they want to come to hear Jesus preach the message of God.

Question 2. Possible responses: fear of being dropped (true of almost all paralyzed people because they can't catch or protect themselves), embarrassment, fear or curiosity about what Jesus might say about this interruption, feeling alone in a crowd (his friends are up on the roof), hope that Jesus will heal him.

Question 3. Note that Jesus lovingly calls him "son," which may have encouraged the man. "Your sins are forgiven" may cause strong positive or negative reactions from members of the group.

Question 4. The teachers of the law are correct: only God can forgive sins. Because of who Jesus is, he has the authority to forgive sins (which he demonstrates immediately after this).

Question 5. Without words being spoken, Jesus knows what they are thinking (note that this is mentioned three times in verses 6 and 8). He teaches that his authority to forgive sins (which are hidden in the heart) is shown by his authority to heal the paralytic (visible before everyone). If Jesus knows the hearts of his accusers he also knows the paralytic's heart and our hearts. Look at the word list to see what Jesus is saying about himself when he uses the title "Son of Man."

Question 6. Jesus saw Levi and spoke to him. When Jesus spoke Levi obeyed and followed. Then Jesus and his disciples ate with Levi and his friends.

Question 7. To follow Jesus means to hear his invitation to get up and follow. Jesus then enters into our lives.

Question 8. Jesus eats with tax collectors and "sinners" because they recognize they are sick with sin and need a "doctor" to be forgiven. Jesus longs to have relationships with people who recognize their spiritual need.

Charting Our Course. The paralytic and Levi were both sick with a deadly and paralyzing disease called *sin.* Sin paralyzes us as well. Jesus wants to heal us, forgive us, and give us new life in relationship with him. He wants to have a party with us.

Study 3. Good News About Evil. Mark 9:14-29.
Purpose: To see that Jesus has authority over evil spirits and that freedom comes through faith and prayer.
General note. This topic might seem unusual for people from the West, but for many other people groups it will be highly relevant.
Introduction. Responses may vary greatly, based on individual experiences or knowledge. Some may doubt the existence of any spirits, while for others evil spirits are very real. The discussion should give you a better understanding of group members' spiritual understanding and needs.
Question 2. If there's a question about Jesus' appearance you can explain that some commentaries suggest that Jesus' appearance changed during the Mount of Transfiguration experience, thus the people were "overwhelmed with wonder" (v. 15), but others point to verse 9, suggesting that Jesus wouldn't order them not to tell anyone if it was so obvious anyway.

Focus on what the people are starting to think about Jesus: he is someone with authority. Even though people love to watch a lively argument, Jesus is far more interesting. Also the father calls Jesus "Teacher," so they may have turned to Jesus as the one who has authority to settle this dispute.
Question 3. The ability to communicate with thoughtful speech and the gift of self-control are some of the things that set people apart from animals. Animals are not able to communicate on the same level; they act out of instinct or training. People have free will. Evil spirits have no other goal than to distort, destroy and ultimately kill the image of God in people.
Question 5. Jesus knows what will happen and is not worried. He wants to help the father recognize his unbelief and understand what reaching out in faith means. Faith means recognizing your own helplessness in an impossible situation and crying out to Jesus for help.

Although there is no specific question on verse 19, some group members may be disturbed by Jesus' words here. Jesus has been telling his disciples about his death and resurrection (Mark 9:9, 12). Knowing that he will leave soon, he wants his disciples to be believing, not unbelieving. "How long shall I put up with you?" may be in the sense of, "How long shall I carry you, bear you, sustain you?"
Question 6. Jesus speaks to a deaf spirit and it hears; he commands it to come out and it does; when everyone thinks the boy is dead, Jesus raises him up. Jesus also knows exactly what kind of spirit the evil spirit is (v. 25) without it telling him (the spirit is mute).

Question 7. Prayer is honest communication with God.

Question 8. Prayer is asking. It's honest about doubts. It's a cry of the heart for help.

Charting Our Course. In order to experience freedom and restoration to wholeness as human beings, we need to say to Jesus, as the father did, "Take pity on us and help us. I do believe; help me overcome my unbelief!" First we must recognize, as the father did, that we're unable to help ourselves. Then we turn to Jesus for help, asking him to deliver and restore us. That's what faith in Jesus is: admitting our inability, recognizing Jesus' ability to do anything, turning to him and asking for his power to change our lives.

Study 4. Good News About Life. John 10:1-21.

Purpose: To see that Jesus came to call and save his people, to lead, nourish and protect them, and to bring them all together into one family and that he gave his life to accomplish this.

Introduction. People motivated by their own gain may even go so far as to kill others. People motivated by love may give their life for others. If group members seem at a loss in thinking of specific people, suggest an enemy who is interested in gain, and suggest their parents as possible people who are motivated by love.

Question 1. The relationship is open and honest (the shepherd goes in by the gate, v. 2), the sheep listen to his voice, he knows his sheep by name, he leads them and they follow. It's a trust relationship.

Question 2. If the group is as baffled as the people in the story, go on to the next question. Some may see that Jesus is saying something about his relationship with those who listen to his voice.

Question 3. Note that Jesus begins this second paragraph as he did the first, with the solemn statement, "I tell you the truth." He wants to emphasize the importance of what he's saying. Jesus is the gate—the way we get in and out, the way we are saved (kept safe). Through him we find nourishment (pasture, v. 9), freedom and life to the fullest. The thieves (all others, v. 8) take away freedom and destroy, following them leads to death.

Question 4. The hired hand cares nothing for the sheep, because he doesn't own them. He cares only for himself, his own safety and his money. The good shepherd owns the sheep and cares so much for them that he will sacrifice his own life to protect them.

Question 5. Jesus lays down his life for the sheep, he brings others that are of a different sheep pen and speaks to them (they listen to his voice), he joins them all together to make one flock, and he shepherds them.

Question 6. The text does not clearly state the answer. Since Jesus is speaking here with Jewish people, "other sheep that are not of this sheep pen" (v. 16) likely refers to non-Jewish peoples who will listen to his voice and be united into one flock under his loving care.

Question 7. The shepherd lays down his life for his sheep because they belong to him and he cares for them (vv. 11-13), and to protect them and keep them together (v. 12).

Question 8. Jesus has authority over life and death!

Question 9. Jesus' claims are jarring in their boldness. There is no room for neutrality about who he is.

Charting Our Course. Jesus is unique. His statements are exclusive. Those who listen will be called by name, be led by the good shepherd (v. 3), be saved, have freedom, find nourishment (v. 9), have life that is full (v. 10), be protected (v. 12), experience Jesus' care (v. 13), be known (v. 14), be brought into one flock (v. 16).

Study 5. Why Did Jesus Die? Luke 23:13-25, 32-56.

Purpose: To understand the events surrounding Jesus' death and the reasons for his death.

Introduction. It can be very emotional for people to recall their feelings about death. Be gentle and a good listener. People may express sadness, anger, frustration, helplessness, injustice or other feelings.

Question 1. Pilate shows that he is an unjust judge, only wanting to please the people. First he offers to punish Jesus (vv. 16 and 22), though he declares that Jesus committed no crime. When the people continue shouting, he gives in to their demand to have Jesus crucified.

Question 2. We could expect anger, bitterness, hate and sarcasm, but instead he forgives.

Question 3. All of these people challenge Jesus' claim about who he really is: "If he is the Christ" (v. 35), "If you are the king" (v. 37) and "Aren't you the Christ?" (v. 39). All of them think they know how he should act: "Save yourself" (vv. 35, 37, 39). Since he doesn't act to save himself, they conclude that his claims are false.

Question 4. The criminal fears God because he realizes that in a very short time they will all die and face God, their holy, pure, just judge.

Question 5. He believes Jesus is innocent (v. 41), that Jesus will live ("remember me" means he believes Jesus will be capable of remembering), that Jesus is a king and has a kingdom which he will rule. Amazing faith in light of the situation on the cross.

Question 6. Jesus has authority to forgive sins. Faith in Jesus gives us a relationship with him, assuring us a place with him in paradise.

Question 7. God is the only explanation for each event: he controls the sun, he tore the curtain of the Jewish temple which separated the people and the most holy place, he can change the heart of a Roman soldier, and he can lead people to repent.

Question 8. Joseph, a member of the council that condemned Jesus to

death, risked rejection, risked losing his place on the council, and risked
death by going to the unjust Pilate. By taking and caring for the body,
Joseph was identifying himself as a follower of Jesus.
Question 9. Jesus was dead. In the warm Middle East, the spices and
perfumes would help preserve the body to keep it from stinking.
Charting Our Course. Some risks might include being rejected by
friends or family, losing your job—or even death.

Study 6. Jesus Is Alive! Luke 24:1-53.

Purpose: To understand the fact that Jesus is alive again and what that
can mean for our lives: forgiveness of sins and great joy.
Introduction. This might be an unexpected good grade on a test, the news
of someone's birth, getting accepted into the university program, receiving
a full scholarship, getting a visa, receiving good news that someone is safe
that you thought was dead and so forth.
General note. This is a long passage so you'll want to focus on the main
events. You may want to read each section separately and answer the
question before going on to the next section.

Jesus' coming back to life is a total surprise for everyone. Even when
told by trusted friends that Jesus is alive, the disciples find it hard to
believe; they watched him die (Luke 23:49).
Question 1. The women were planning to put the spices on the body to
help keep it from stinking. They went during the early hours before the
day's heat (the cool air helps keep the smell down). They expected the stone
to cover the tomb and the body to be there. Instead they found the stone
rolled away, the body gone (vv. 2-3) and two men with gleaming clothes
who told them Jesus is alive (vv. 5-7).
Question 2. The women observed the facts and believed. They went back
and told all the others. The men didn't believe the women but thought it
was nonsense. Peter ran to the empty tomb, saw the strips of linen that
Jesus' body had been wrapped in, and wondered what happened.
Question 3. Jesus was a prophet, powerful in word and deed before God
and all the people (v. 19), and was now dead (v. 20). They had hoped he was
the one who was going to redeem Israel (v. 21).
Question 4. First the women had told them about the morning, but they
didn't believe them (vv. 22-24) even though some of the men went to the
tomb and found it just as the women had said. They knew the facts but
didn't believe them, so Jesus said to them, "How foolish you are!" (v. 25).
Next Jesus took them to the words of God recorded by Moses and all the
prophets (v. 27). Then they invited Jesus in to stay with them (v. 29). As
they ate with him (v. 30) their eyes were opened and they recognized him.
We too need to study God's Word, invite Jesus in and have fellowship with
him. Then he opens our eyes to really see him.

According to verse 35, they recognized Jesus when he broke the bread. Perhaps this was because they saw his nail-scarred hands, or they were reminded of how Jesus celebrated his last supper with them (Luke 22:7-20) or of the way Jesus prayed (v. 30).

Question 5. Jesus begins with questions, helps them think and respond (v. 38), and shows them that he knows what they are thinking and understands their fears and doubts. Then he invites them to look (visual evidence) and touch him (tactile evidence) (v. 39). He reasons with them (intellectual evidence) pointing out that ghosts don't have flesh and bones (v. 39). He eats (which ghosts can't do) and then presents evidence from prophecy in Scripture (vv. 44-45).

Question 6. Now the message can be preached to people of all nations: we can repent (turn around) and receive forgiveness for our sins (v. 47).

Charting Our Course. Because these are very personal questions, some people in your group may hesitate to answer, which is okay. The steps that can be taken are the same ones we've been reading about: express doubts and fears and ask questions, listen to the words of others who speak about Jesus (vv. 6-7, 9), read the Scriptures, and invite Jesus himself to answer the doubts and open our minds to understand the Scriptures (vv. 27, 45). If we invite Jesus in to stay with us (v. 29), he will open our eyes.

PART FOUR: Experiencing God
Study 1. Responding to God. Luke 8:4-9, 11-15.
Purpose: To consider how we have responded or are responding to God's message.

General note. Verse 10 is intentionally avoided so as to keep the continuity of the story of the soils and not create a possibly confusing tangent for people new to the Bible.

Question 1. You may wish to illustrate these types of soil from your own spiritual journey. Your experience may help participants realize that soil types can change.

Question 3. Avoid a tangent, but point out that the devil is active in keeping people from God. There are spiritual powers opposed to truth.

Question 5. Listen carefully to answers to this question. You may discover obstacles in other cultures which are uncommon to your experience. This question also helps the participants think about this parable as it applies to their cultural context.

Question 7. Materialism is an issue for all people. In some cultures it manifests itself in consumerism, while in others it shows up in wealth-building or savings.

Question 10. Allow time for people to think about this question and to describe their own experience as they are comfortable.

Study 2. A Working Man Responds. Luke 5:1-11.

Purpose: To see that realizing we are sinners is the first step in becoming a follower of Jesus.

Getting Oriented. Change is always intimidating. Recall the fear and concerns of change, but also recall the positive results. This discussion may help people put into perspective the possibility of following Jesus. It involves change and perhaps some fears, but the results will bring joy and purpose as we enter into relationship with God.

Question 1. It appears "accidental"—Jesus needs a boat, and Simon has one.

Question 3. Simon was probably proud to let Jesus use his boat, but now Jesus is telling him how and when to fish. It was the common practice to fish in the evening or early morning. If no fish had been caught in the evening, the probability of catching fish at this hour was nil. Simon thought he knew more about fishing than Jesus did. But because he respected Jesus, Simon did as he said—with very low expectations.

Question 7. Jesus often says "don't be afraid." He is the friend of sinful people, not their enemy.

Charting Our Course. Following Jesus as Lord could have varied implications for people. Connect this question with the question in "Getting Oriented."

Study 3. A Rich Person Responds. Luke 18:18-30.

Purpose: To communicate that following Jesus takes both faith and action. There is a cost involved in becoming a follower of Jesus.

Question 3. He understands human nature. He knows that we can rationalize our behavior or try to serve two masters.

Question 4. The ruler had asked what he must *do,* so Jesus refers to the commands that are primarily action-oriented. The ruler obviously did not reflect on the heart attitudes that are addressed in commandments one and ten. He has a very superficial understanding of what God requires.

Question 5. He reveals that he doesn't understand the commandments and what they require. His wealth was more important to him than the treasure God gives.

Question 6. It was the common idea of the day that material wealth was a sign of God's favor.

Question 7. The commandments are impossible for any to keep, so eternal life cannot be earned. Yet eternal life can be experienced because God offers it as a gift.

Question 9. If you are the only follower of Jesus in your group, you may wish to share your experiences of both leaving some things behind and receiving God's gifts of replacement.

Study 4. An International Visitor Responds. Acts 8:26-39.

Purpose: To encourage the seeker to ask questions about the Bible and to realize that God is pursuing a love relationship with us.

General note. This study was written for people who are actively responding to God's initiative in their life. Be sensitive to people in the group who may be ready to embrace the Good News.

Question 3. He is an active reader who is trying to understand what he is reading.

Question 4. It speaks of death, not victory. This contradicts the image of a triumphant Savior or Messiah.

Question 5. The resurrection is the missing piece of the story and would put it all in perspective. Philip also no doubt explained how Jesus bore our sins.

Question 6. God has made good on his ancient promises. We can be saved from our sins.

Question 8. Philip willingly crossed a cultural barrier and approached a stranger. He never pushed his ideas but responded to the Ethiopian's questions. He obviously tries to base the man's confidence in God and the Bible rather than in himself.

Charting Our Course. If the group members don't see themselves as responding to God's initiative, then help them see that their presence in this study is one step toward God. Help them think how they could apply something to their own lives—for example, to be thankful for what they have learned about God.

Study 5. A Military Officer Responds. Acts 10:1-48.

Purpose: To see that the good news of Jesus is for all cultures and all people.

General note. This passage is longer than most. You may wish to divide it into two separate studies. Break at 10:23 since there was a two-day interval at this point. Focus on Cornelius' thoughts and feelings to create a degree of anticipation.

Question 4. Leviticus 11 spells out the prohibitions, and Peter was in the habit of following God's law. His whole understanding of God was now challenged.

Question 5. People may mention such customs as taking shoes off at the door, not shaking a woman's hand, covering the head while praying, not eating certain meats.

Question 6. He willingly greeted his Gentile visitors and invited them to stay overnight.

Question 7. He had invited friends and relatives in anticipation of Peter's arrival. He expected an important message from God via Peter.

Questions 8-9. No human is inherently unclean. God is God for every nation, and belief in Jesus is the basis for cleanliness.

Question 10. Verse 35 notes that "every nation" is accepted and verse 43 says "everyone."

Question 12. Verse 35 appears to suggest that people can be acceptable based on their works, but then there would be no need for Cornelius to hear Peter's message, for he was devout and God-fearing. Verse 43 shows that those who believe receive forgiveness, and the baptism in verse 48 is a sign of the new life for those who believe.

Study 6. An Outcast Woman Responds. John 4:1-30, 39-42.

Purpose: To realize that no one is an outcast from God. His love reaches out to every one of us.

Question 1. It was the practice of Jews not to drink from a cup that had been used by someone considered "unclean," such as the Samaritans. A man encountering a woman who was a stranger to him did not usually engage her in conversation. Jesus was breaking cultural, religious and gender norms by asking this woman for a drink.

Question 2. You might give examples from your immediate context (the school cafeteria, housing areas in your city, and so on).

Question 3. Jesus is speaking of spiritual things; the woman is speaking of earthly things.

Question 6. It would be normal for the village women to gather early, before the heat of the day, to draw water. Perhaps she was unwelcome among the village women because of her reputation, and so she drew her water alone at a time when no one would be at the well.

Charting Our Course. Many people thirst for acceptance. Coming home to our true Father through Jesus will provide the ultimate acceptance we so desperately want.

Depending on your circumstances, you may wish to offer people an opportunity to become part of God's family. Give them time to read the section titled "The Final Word" and to pray the prayer if they wish.